COASTAL
ANGLING
GUIDE

COASTAL ANGLING GUIDE

Tom Schlichter

Cartoons and line drawings by Bobbie Ludwig

NORTHEAST SPORTSMAN'S PRESS
TARRYTOWN, NEW YORK

STACKPOLE BOOKS
HARRISBURG, PENNSYLVANIA

Library of Congress Cataloging in Publication Data

Schlichter, Tom.
    Coastal angling guide / Tom Schlichter ; cartoons and line
drawings by Bobbie Ludwig.
      p.   cm.
    ISBN 0-8117-4015-3 : $12.95
    1. Fishing – Atlantic Coast (U.S.)   I. Title.
SH464.A85S35   1989
799.1'6614 – dc20   89-8561

Portions of this book appeared in Tom Schlichter's earlier book,
Northeast Party Boat Fishing.

Principal Photography by the author.

Recipes created, tested and compiled with the generous assistance of
Tina Schlichter.

Design by Jim Capossela
Cover design by Art Unlimited

Published by Stackpole Books and Northeast Sportsmans Press
Distributed by Stackpole Books
Cameron & Kelker Streets
P.O. Box 1831
Harrisburg, Pennsylvania 17105

Printed in the United States of America
10-9-8-7-6-5-4-3-2-1

ACKNOWLEDGEMENTS

A book of this nature requires input, advice, suggestions and support from a wide variety of sources. I consider myself extremely lucky to have found so many people ready and willing to pitch in and lend a hand. It is great to see that the camaraderie which exists on the water is also present on dry land.

First of all, I would like to extend my thanks to the many party and charter boat skippers who offered their encouragement, knowledge and in some cases, photos. Especially helpful were:

Capt. John Alberta, *Sound Charters* in Huntington, NY
Capt. Howard Bogan, *The Jamaica* in Brielle, NJ
Capt. Dave Brennan, the *Peconic Star* in Greenport, NY
Capt. Brad Glass, the *Hel-Cat* in Groton, CT
Capt. Matt Hazan, the *Sherlock* in Mt. Sinai, NY
Capt. Paul G. Fosberg, the *Viking Fleet* in Montauk, NY
Capt. Charlie Kennedy, the *Capt. Joseph* in Captree, NY
Capt. Hank Leonard, the *Golden Eagle* in Belmar, NJ
Capt. Tim Tower, the *Bunny Clark* in Ogunquit, ME

For general information and expert advice on hook sizes and rigging, the crew at J&J Bait and Tackle in Patchogue, NY, went beyond the call of duty, as did many Sea Grant Specialists and Cornell Cooperative Extension Agents along the Atlantic coast.

My publisher, Jim Capossela, also deserves a word of thanks. His occasional reminders to keep my nose to the grindstone, and his expressions of confidence in my abilities as a writer, greatly boosted my determination to bring this project to completion.

To my parents, who took the time to get me started in fishing and encouraged me to write, offering support of every kind along the way, I extend a loving thank you.

Finally, I would like to thank my wife Tina for her willingness to type and proofread the text under deadline pressure, and express my gratitude to both her and my daughter Corrine for their unwavering support of me despite the time I had to take from them while working on this book. There is nothing more precious than time spent with family, and it will take a few summers until it's paid back in full.

In loving memory of my dad,
Robert Matthew Schlichter, Sr.,
who turned each trip we took together
into a wonderful learning experience.

The author and his father, shown with the latter's 65-pound codfish.
Taken on a special wreck-fishing trip aboard the Viking Star out of
Montauk, New York, this giant cod won a $1680 pool. Photo taken
May 27, 1980.

ILLUSTRATIONS

Chapter	Number	Description	
Eight	8a.	Tandem-Tied Flounder Rig	83
Nine	9a.	Standard Bottom Rig	91
Eleven	11a.	Jelly Worm For Weakfish	111
Twelve	12a.	Standard Fluke Rig	115
	12b.	Lead Head And Squid Strip	118
	12c.	Slip Sinker Rig For Fluke Or Flounder	123
Thirteen	13a.	High-Low Rig	129
Fifteen	15a.	Codfish Rig With Teaser	139
Sixteen	16a.	Mackerel Tree	148
Nineteen	19a.	Popular Hook Styles	172
	19b.	Hook Points	173
	19c.	Clinch Knot	174
	19d.	Improved Clinch Knot	174
	19e.	Dropper Loop	175
	19f.	End Loop	176
Twenty	20a.	Sample From Author's Log Book	181

CONTENTS

PART I—BASICS FOR THE PRIVATE BOATER
Chapter 1   Choosing Your Boat 3
Chapter 2   The Personal Touch:
             Outfitting For Fishing 15
Chapter 3   General Thoughts On Tackle 25
Chapter 4   Fitting In: Safety Rules And The
             Unwritten Codes 38

PART II—THE PARTY BOAT GAME
Chapter 5   Welcome Aboard 48
Chapter 6   Finding And Choosing Boats 53
Chapter 7   Strategies, Tackle And Other Insights 61

PART III—THE QUARRY AND THE TECHNIQUE
Chapter 8   Winter Flounder 78
Chapter 9   Blackfish (Tautog) 87
Chapter 10   Striped Bass (Rockfish) 94
Chapter 11   Weakfish & Sea Trout 105
Chapter 12   Fluke (Summer Flounder) 114
Chapter 13   Porgies And Seabass 125
Chapter 14   Whiting and Ling 132
Chapter 15   Codfish 137
Chapter 16   Mackerel 146
Chapter 17   Bluefish 151

PART IV—ODDS AND ENDS
Chapter 18   Some Thoughts On Charters and Rentals 162
Chapter 19   Hooks And Knots:
             Making The Best Choice 170
Chapter 20   The Value Of A Logbook 178
Chapter 21   Proper Fish Care 187
Chapter 22   Delicious Fish Recipes 190

Part I:
Basics For
The Private
Boater

It starts innocently enough, the addiction to fishing. Perhaps a trip with dad to a local dock, maybe a day spent on a party boat with a few friends or a solitary venture to the ocean surf where the brilliance of a rising sun can best be observed. In any case the end result is the same: a burning desire to go again and again. As quickly as his first fish is held aloft for all the world to see, the angler too is solidly hooked. In the long run, the fish has the better chance of escaping.

For the angler, boats are a natural extension of the desire to catch more and bigger fish. There's a special satisfaction, a feeling of self-sufficiency, that one gets when dinner is gathered from a private craft. But there's more to this sport than simply filling a cooler. The boating angler attains a degree of freedom the bank fisherman can only dream about. Untethered to the shore, a captain can roam the coastline in search of his quarry and fight his game on more equal terms. He can take the battle to the fish rather than hope the schools chance by. He can use lighter tackle and different methods or be more selective in the kind of fish he pursues. It's a more active kind of fishing than casting from the bank.

Of course, with new freedoms come new questions and responsibilities. What type of boat will you need and how should you set it up for fishing? What tackle and methods will work best in the waters you will try? You'll have to be concerned with other boats, navigation and the safety of your passengers. With a little preparation, though, these concerns should be easy to handle. The following section should get you started on your way.

Chapter 1

⚓

Choosing Your Boat

With the exception of the complete novice, most anglers are generally comfortable when it comes to buying new tackle, hooks, lures, and other fishing related items. The purchase of a boat, however, is a completely different story, often raising anxiety levels even in the most experienced fishermen. Buying a boat, even a small, used model, is a major financial investment for most of us. Thus, its a good idea to do a little research before making a deal.

FINANCING A BOAT PURCHASE

Having the choice, it's a fair bet that most anglers would like to start out with a brand new vessel. Impossible, you say? Maybe not. There are a wide range of craft in the $5,000 to $15,000 price range that can serve well the needs of most east coast fishermen. With today's financing plans and your own good credit rating, some dealers may even be able to make your dreams come true with "no money down" deals while keeping monthly installments somewhat reasonable. The catch, of course, is long term payments to the bank. It's up to you to decide if such a protracted contract is justifiable.

While many people simply go to their local bank for boat loans, there are some lending institutions which specialize in boat financing and these may have better rates than commercial banks. You can find these institutions advertising in local fishing or boating magazines, or working the winter boat shows. They might be worth speaking with. If you are inexperienced in finances, it might also be advisable to speak with an accountant or other money professional before entering any agreements.

Can you afford the monthly payments? If so that's a good start, but before signing on the dotted line consider some of the other bills that will come with your new toy: dock fees, fuel, service, taxes, insurance, winter storage and an emergency fund for those unexpected expenditures that never fail to arise as the season progresses. Add these costs up and you'll quickly realize that owning a boat can take a good bite out of one's paycheck.

With the above in mind, it should come as no surprise that, despite the existence of creative financing, not everyone buys a new boat the first (or even second or third) time around. In fact, most boat buyers probably purchase a used craft listed in the local classifieds or perched high and dry on a neighborhood front lawn, a "For Sale" sign dangled over the bow. The advantage to buying a used boat most notably is low price but finding one that has already been set up specifically for fishing can be a tremendous plus. Whether you buy new or used, however, things are likely to prove most satisfying if you first put some serious thought into deciding exactly what type of vessel will best suit your needs from family, fishing and monetary points of view.

Will you fish mostly in protected bays or harbors or will you bee-line for the inlets and open seas? If you feel there is some ocean fishing in your future, will it be done within a mile or two of the beach or out over deep water and far away from normal boating traffic? Is bottom fishing your game or do you prefer to troll or cast plugs? Will the family be coming along from time to time? How heavy a boat can your car comfortably tow? These are the kind of questions that must go into the final analysis, the answers to each shaping and molding your thoughts on the ideal craft. Regardless if the boat you are considering is worth $500 or $25,000, it warrants a thorough going over before any transactions are completed. A test ride, if at all possible, is also in order.

CHOOSING A BOAT TO FIT YOUR NEEDS
Family and monetary considerations aside, the starting point for picking a fishing boat, new or used, should center around determining the kind of hull design which will best lend itself to your particular style of fishing and the waters you'll most often work. For most anglers, this

Outboard Problems?

Today's high-tech, fuel efficient outboards are much more reliable than their predecessors of only a few years ago. Still, just about every boat owner eventually needs to make a stop at the local outboard service center and that usually means shelling out at least a hundred bucks. Following is a list of some of the most frequent reasons why outboard engines are brought in for repair, and the typical charges for them. The charges below are for an 85 horsepower outboard engine and include both parts and labor. Going labor rates vary between $45 and $65 an hour. Note that prices can differ considerably, even within the same town, so it pays to shop around.

Service	Charge
1. Tune-up and replace spark plugs	$75-$100
2. Thermostat replacement	$90-$110
3. Aluminum prop (customer installed)	$90-$120
4. Winterize motor	$90-$120
5. Replace water pump	$160-$190
6. Replace electronic power pack module	$190-$210
7. Rebuild carburetor	$240-$310
8. Complete replacement and reseal of lower unit gear cases	$400-$550

What can you do to keep your engine running smoothly and avoid a visit to the repairman? Most experts agree that more than anything else, using a high quality outboard oil with a BIA or MMAC approved rating, such as TCWII, will help the most. Other hints include changing the gear oil at least twice a year, spraying down the power head and electronics with a quality spray lubricant that will not erode neoprene hoses (CRC 666 is a good choice), and using a gas stabilizer (such as MDR Store and Start or OMC 2+4 fuel conditioner) a few times a year to help keep the fuel system clean. Oh, yes—avoiding sand bars while under power helps, too!

will mean deciding among four basic styles: modified-vee, tri-hull, flat bottomed or deep-vee.

The modified-vee style is easily the most popular hull design among the inshore crowd. Typical of this design are the 19 foot Mako, 16 foot Privateer, and a slew of similar 17 to 21 foot dry riding, center, side

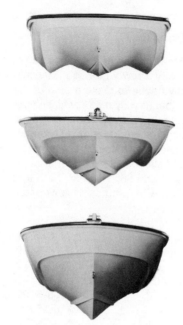

Three basic hull styles favored by inshore fishermen are from top to bottom: tri-hull, modified-vee and deep-vee. Each manufacturer has its own variations on these themes.

and dual consoles so popular these days. An excellent choice for bay, inlet or inshore ocean fishing (to about 20 miles offshore for some boats of 23 feet or more), this hull features a wide and stable bow with moderate draft allowing it to brave the often turbulent waters of inlets or rips (albeit at half throttle) while still riding high enough to sneak into river eddies, shallow coves or skinny water back bay flats where owners of larger boats or deep-vee style hulls dare not trespass. Better yet, because of their relatively moderate sizes and weights, these boats usually trailer easily behind most mid-sized cars. The modified-vee is at it's best on windless days when the seas lay low, for it is then that these craft can show off their speed and impressive fuel economy while boasting but moderate sized outboards. In fact, many of the modified-vees I've seen on the water in recent years have been over-matched by their horses. While speed is often desirable, too much power can be wasteful or, worse, dangerous. Like fishing tackle, a boat and its motor should be evenly balanced.

Although speed, economy and ease of ride are often-touted advantages of the modified-vee, I would be remiss if I failed to point out that all three of these advantages are greatly reduced when a solid chop of two and a half feet or more develops. At such times you'll have to back down on the throttle to avoid rattling your teeth as the boat pounds hard across the wave tops. Still, for overall versatility under a wide range of sea conditions this hull style is hard to beat. Luckily, recent design improvements by some manufacturers have begun to ease the bumpiness out of choppy water riding, especially in the larger of these boats.

The tri-hull design, most often associated with the smaller Boston Whaler style boats, offers a reassuringly sturdy and balanced deck, ideal for the back bay angler or those who generally work relatively mild waters. This is a great hull style for casting or poling situations, though it rides considerably rougher than does the modified-vee in anything more than a slight chop. If you like to stand and cast, however, the stability of this craft in the 16 foot range is hard to overlook and these boats have the added advantage of riding very dry most of the time. Like modified-vees, most tri-hulls are easily trailered.

Next, we have the flat bottom hull style of "tin boat" fame. These see but limited use in most salt water situations, yet for those who fish solely in protected waters, its cheap price, small size and easy transportability may be just what the doctor ordered. The smallest of these boats are often "cartopped" while larger craft require a small trailer but are still light enough to be towed by even a tiny import car. Obviously, with their flat bottoms and small size (mostly between 10 and 14 feet) these boats are built for neither speed nor comfort and their range is quite limited by their generally lightweight motors, or by choppy or turbulent waters or gusty winds. On the plus side, the small outboards, usually between 6 and 25 horsepower, are relatively inexpensive and allow anglers to quietly approach sheltered hotspots with a minimum of disturbance and noise. Best of all, these boats can be slipped into the water from virtually any accessible stretch of beach.

The deep-vee hull style is a little beyond the scope of this book as it is used mostly by ocean-going sailors who spend more time chasing down blue water predators than prospecting for the relatively shallow feeders to be covered here. Still, it should be noted that anglers who continually work rough rips or turbulent inlet areas might find the excellent maneuverability and ease with which this hull slices through the water to be an advantage over the modified-vee. This is especially true for those who like to troll, since the pounding of a modified hull as it bounces from wavecrest to wavecrest while cruising the length of a sluiceway or heavy rip can be a little trying.

The choice of motor for any of the above will pretty much fall in line with the size and style of hull selected. In fact, most dealers offer the engine as part of a package, often including a suitable pre-selected trailer as well. Even in package deals, though, there can be some flexibility.

Although some of these boats may be able to accommodate inboard or inboard/outboard motors, less expensive conventional outboards are the usual choice for boats of 12 to 23 feet. While outboard fuel economy ratings do not quite match those of the below-deck-based power plants, today's new models are quite adequate and their behind-the-stern placement allows better utilization of space in the form of stow-away areas, live wells or fish boxes. Additionally, an outboard can be tilted to expose the prop while on the water, allowing one to easily remove any kind of fouled matter or to drift off a sandbar when accidentally grounded -- both occasional happenings where inshore boating is concerned. On the downside, outboards tend to be a lot noisier, easier to foul a line on, and slightly less dependable in general -- especially in cool weather -- than inboards or I/O's.

No matter what kind of motor you decide on (a few other variations are available) keep the following two rules in mind when reaching a decision: 1) Buy an established brand for which replacement parts are widely available; and 2) Make sure there is more than one service center for that brand engine within a reasonable distance from your boat slip or home. Why two service centers? Well, it seems to me they are just like car service centers and prices and quality of work can vary widely from one establishment to the next. With a minimum of two centers nearby, at least you've got a little choice.

Once the hull and engine debate has been put to rest, you'll next need to consider the on-deck layout of your future dream machine. While anglers with cartop sized boats will usually have to settle for a side console or even a steering lever attached to the motor, those looking at boats of 14 feet or more will have several choices. The larger the craft the more the available options. In general, you'll have to pick from a menu of center console, side console, dual console, or cuddy cabin. In the right situation, each can prove quite appetizing.

Currently, the center console is the runaway favorite layout of America's inshore salt water boater and it's easy to see why. This design allows concentration of all essential navigational and electronic fish finding equipment while offering the major plus of 360-degree walk-around pathways. It is also relatively inexpensive, since it requires minimum tooling and construction materials. On boats of less than 21 feet, where lack of space is often a major concern, the center console is the answer to a captain's prayers, providing all the above benefits while also serving to support fishing poles stored in rod holders. Whether fighting big game or small, a panicked fish can be easily followed from stern to bow and back again -- even if it moves from port to starboard.

Sound too good to be true? Well, there is a two-fold downside to center consoles. First, if you fish in an area where it gets cold you're liable to freeze your buns off getting to and from the fishing grounds. With no cabin there is little protection from the elements. Although a T-top may be added to the console and a pull-up canvas positioned at the bow, the driver is protected by nothing more than a small plexiglass windshield and the console itself. Second, LCD (Liquid Crystal Display) monitors positioned within the console will often be "washed out" by the sun, since there is little or nothing overhead to keep glare off their screens. Even with a T-top, a bright, sunny day will take the contrast out of most monitors currently on the market.

Side consoles are often featured on smaller boats where a center console would simply be impractical. While requiring a minimum of construction and wiring, they do not lend themselves well to holding rods and often do not have enough width, length or heighth to allow easy installation of electronic fish finding or navigational gear. The small boat

COURTESY GRUMMAN CORP.

Small flat-bottomed or modified-vee aluminum boats are ideal for working quiet backwater areas.

operator can probably overlook these limitations since most small boaters are not fully up on electronic gadgetry, but there is still another disadvantage to this setup -- it puts the driver closer to the spray as the boat powers along. In anything more than a light chop it's difficult to stay dry with this arrangement -- even at slow speeds -- and a following sea usually means a good drenching. Nonetheless, because of its low price and simplicity, a large number of small boats feature this floor plan.

The dual console layout was quite popular before the center console came along and stole the limelight, but I'm told this style setup is currently enjoying a slight comeback. With more and more electronics available to the angler, the dual console offers plenty of space to put a VHF-radio, compass, LCD or what have you. Better yet, these devices will be positioned below and behind the front windshield where they should stay relatively dry during your trip. Positioned near the bow, dual consoles also sport plenty of free room aft of the helm and lend themselves well to pull-up canvas tops, which with a clear plastic viewing front allows the driver and passengers a good look at water ahead while keeping them dry and out of wind's way. On boats of less than 21 feet, the dual console usually sports a flip-up windshield between the two consoles. This affords extra protection from the elements and can be easily opened to provide quick access to the bow. You'll pay a little extra for the dual console layout, however, and working a fish around the consoles may be inconvenient at times, especially if you're fishing with a canvas top secured in place.

The cuddy cabin style layout features an enclosed cockpit and of the different deck styles presented here, affords the most comfort for captain and crew. Unfortunately, it's practical only on larger craft. The cabin area on a full cuddy runs from gunwale to gunwale, offering spacious accommodations for electronics, room in the bow for bunks and/or storage (depending on the size of the boat), and, if combined with a hardtop or 360-degree canvas, almost full protection from the elements. The increasingly popular walk-around cuddy offers the above on a smaller, tighter scale, with paths outside and adjacent to the cabin providing access to the topside bow. For the fisherman, this means easier access to the front of the vessel when fighting a big fish or securing an anchor line, etc. Aside from the obvious limitations of "going up front", cuddy cabins run several thousand dollars more than do the other layouts.

Center consoles concentrate helm options, electronics, fish and storage boxes, and even spare rod holders just slightly aft of midship, leaving anglers plenty of room for fighting fish or just walking around the boat.

Provided you've selected a vessel appropriate for your kind of fishing, and assuming you've bought the boat from a reputable dealer, you shouldn't have too much to worry about as your maiden voyage approaches. After all, one year warranties are standard on most motors, 90-day warranties cover most of the electronics and accessories while the hull should be covered for a minimum of one to three years for a fiberglass or compound based boat and as much as 5 to 20 years for aluminum craft. All should be in working order as the boat is delivered or picked up and a good once over should reveal no surprises. For the first season or two, you should have few if any mechanical or electrical problems to deal with. If any do arise, the dealer or manufacturer should be able to help you out.

TIPS FOR THE USED BOAT BUYER

If you are planning to purchase a used boat you must exercise a little extra caution before shaking on a deal. Used boats need to be evaluated not only for their future tasks, but also in the context of their previous usage. The new boat buyer will find virtually any hull on the market to be constructed of fiberglass or some new, space-age compound. These are almost always in good condition as they leave the dealer. The used boat buyer, on the other hand, will have to choose among hulls made of fiberglass, compounds or even wood. Many times, a close inspection will reveal the kind of hidden damage that the new boat buyer need not fear.

In general, wood hulled boats run less expensive than fiberglass ones but what you save in cost you'll probably make up for in the time and elbow grease expended to keep such a craft in top condition. When inspecting a wooden boat beware of loose or peeling paint and varnish. This in itself is not necessarily bad, except that it will have to be stripped, sanded and refinished in order to maintain good looks and resistance to the elements. The question is, how much work are you willing to put in? Stripping a boat may not be worth the effort.

Hull planking which is loose may indicate that the fastenings have deteriorated and open seams between planks may point to warping or loss of caulking. Cracked or broken ribs or frames are another concern, and boats with plywood hulls must be checked for delamination which often appears as "bubbles" in the plywood around which there is no evidence of rot. Fixing or replacing one or two ribs or planks is not overly expensive or time consuming, but the task seems to grow geometrically if several need attention.

Rot is a warning sign that should be carefully heeded. Sometimes, a small bit of rot will appear to be confined to a single board or plank. More often, however, finding any rot at all is a good indication that more is lurking somewhere within the hull or transom. Soft, wet and crumbling wood are obvious signs. More subtle tip-offs include small bubbles in the paint or varnish and fungi growing on the exterior surface of the wood. The "quarter test" is a quick way of checking suspect areas of planks, beams or hulls. Simply pull a quarter from your pocket and press it into the section you suspect may be rotted. If the wood is softer than surrounding areas of the same type of wood, anticipate a problem.

There is one more sticky point about small to medium sized wooden boats that prospective buyers should be aware of: they are virtually impossible to insure. This may be no big deal for someone who loses a small skiff, but if your $5000 prize sinks to the bottom, *you* may be sunk. If you are thinking of buying a wooden boat worth more than a grand, it might be a good idea to check with your insurance dealer first.

Fiberglass boats require far, far less maintenance than do wood models, but even these are far from self-maintaining. Fiberglass hulls can be distorted by improper support, poor construction, inadequate reinforcement or poorly made repairs. Look such craft over carefully for cracks in the outer hull, an uneven bottom or a twisted keel. All should serve as caution signs. In the case of cracks, it should be noted that small hairline cracks scattered randomly throughout the outer gel-coat do not indicate a problem unless they extend into the layers of fiberglass underneath. These cracks are often caused because the gel was sprayed on too thickly when the boat was first built. Deeper cracks, however, should be investigated both inside and out. Evidence of past repairs should also be inspected -- non-matching gel coat or sanded, retouched areas are dead giveaways.

On any used boat, special care should be taken to inspect the electrical system, cockpit and interior. Examine all the hatches, ports and coolers to see if they open, close and lock properly. Check to determine if the seals are in good condition and feel around for mildew, rot and dampness. These signs can point toward a leaking hatch or other problem which allows water entry. Are the hardware and fastenings in good condition? Better check before laying out hard-earned cash. Cleats, railings, screws, bolts, fittings and fastenings can be expensive. You might be able to tolerate a little corrosion, but extensive deterioration means that they will soon need to be replaced.

In terms of the electrical system, look over wires and connectors for corrosion, especially male and female connectors and the wires that attach to the battery. Try each light switch and the bilge pump to see that it works. The latter is one item that is rarely repaired before a boat is put up for sale. Check the compass, fish finder or depth recorder and radio if they are part of the package.

Often, a faulty motor is the main reason a boat has been put up for sale. At all costs, try to have the owner run the motor for several minutes before making a final commitment. If the boat is dry docked, an outboard engine can be started in a garbage can full of water. Or better yet, get one of those hose attachments which when screwed on a hose and placed over the lower unit will allow the engine to run cool even in gear. This is the time to check the water pump; it should push the water out with some force. A trickle usually indicates a replacement will be necessary and is good for knocking a hundred dollars or so off the purchase price. How does the engine sound at differing speeds? Does it sputter at idle or low speeds? If it seems a little rough, the seller might insist that nothing more than a "small adjustment" is needed. Ask him to make the correction right then and there. After all, it's just "a little turn of the screw", right?

Engine evaluations should also include a look at the prop to check for broken or cracked blades and severely nicked edges. Either will likely require replacement of the prop. Examine, too, the engine head for peeling paint, a sign of overheating. Finally, if you are thinking of buying any boat motor, purchase a compression gauge and give the motor a compression test. This will help tell the tale of the motor's innards, for an engine with bad rings and worn pistons is virtually worthless. If the engine seems suspect in any major area, it's probably best to look for another deal -- even if the boat hull and electronics are in good shape.

Chapter 2

⚓

The Personal Touch: Outfitting For Fishing

Whether a boat is purchased new or used, it's going to need a little bit of outfitting to give it that personalized, fisherman's touch. This is where individual creativity enters the game. From bare bones setups with nothing more than a couple of home-made rod holders and portable cooler to classic customized outfits sporting fish boxes, live wells, stow-away boxes and the latest in electronic gadgetry, each craft is tailored to suit its style, available space and the fishing habits of its owner.

When it comes to outfitting, there is one rule that holds true for almost any kind of fishing boat: Make efficient use of space. Quite simply, the more open space that is left over when your boat is rigged and ready to go, the better. Never lose sight of the fact that a clean, tidy craft is a joy to ride on or fish from while a disorganized boat cluttered with scattered fishing poles, hooks, tackle, and other fishing debris is an accident waiting to happen -- and accidents on the water have a nasty way of quickly turning serious.

What do you *really* have room for on your fishing boat? That's the question to begin with as you plan to install those finishing touches. The more room to start with, the more luxuries that can be added.

Certainly, storage holders for fishing rods should be at the top of the list if they didn't come with the boat you've just purchased. Nothing puts a damper on a fishing trip quicker than a broken rod tip or reel foot and as long as there are fishing rods laying around on deck, such mishaps are destined to occur. Rod holders and racks also keep poles secure and out of the way, reducing the chances of free swinging hooks imbedding themselves in human flesh.

On most boats, simple rod holders are strategically positioned at the stern and possibly near midship or the bow. In addition to holders used when actually fishing, larger craft may have room below the gunwale or inside the cabin for rod racks to keep your fishing sticks tucked away on long treks. Center console outfits may also position rod holders along the outsides of the console, aft of the driver's seat, or at the rear end of a T-top. Don't be conservative when deciding how many rod holders to put in place; I can't ever recall fishing on a boat that had too many. Imagine going out with three other people and everyone shows up at dockside with only *two* rods apiece; that's eight holders filled in a hurry. And some of your friends are bound to show up with three or four rods.

While rod holders and rod racks are relatively inexpensive, building your own is even less costly and not much trouble at all. The do-it-yourself crowd will find that holders are easily made from 12-inch sections of PVC or ABS tubing fastened vertically to the inside of the boat at the stern, bow or midship. Be sure to position the stern rod holders at an angle conducive to trolling or drifting; a 60 to 70 degree angle to the water seems about right. Other holders usually work best if positioned so that they hold their rods upright.

Self-made rod racks are also easily designed. For these, several sections of four-inch PVC tubing can be fastened horizontally to the inside of the boat below the gunwale. These will hold the tip sections of your rods. To keep the butt ends from bouncing around, position a wooden rack with J-shaped slots at the opposite end of the storage area, four to five feet from the tubes depending on the size rods to be supported. For small dories or tin boats, where there is no room at all for racks, a pair of Velcro straps strategically secured to opposite benches can be used to keep rods, gaffs, etc. in place.

Every boat needs some place to tuck away extra clothes, tackle, boat lines, anchors, tools, raingear, and so on, and for this stow-away boxes are the way to go. Thoughtfully designed to fit beneath, alongside, in front of or even behind benches, seats or consoles, these storage com-

Placing spare rods in holders or racks will keep them safe from damage and out of the way. Here, three setups sit safe and sound tight to the side of a center console.

partments can be store-bought or custom made. A good one will keep extra items relatively dry and out of the way until needed while doubling as a bench or seat. A poorly constructed box will merely keep things out of the way. (In a pinch, a strong cooler works quite well and usually proves more water-tight than most home-made boxes.)

Stow-away boxes can be permanently secured in place, or fastened temporarily with bungee cords, straps and floor brackets, or even Velcro backing. The bow, stern and gunwale are natural places for small boxes while larger ones can be placed amidship. Secure a cushion to the box top and you'll have an extra seat or two. For storing frequently needed tools, lures or other small items, add a pull-out drawer along the bow, gunwale or under the console.

If you plan on building your own stow-away boxes, be advised that it is almost impossible to make one that is water tight or that will even keep dampness out overnight. Still, fair results can be had using one-half to one-inch marine grade plywood, waterproof glue, and corner braces or dovetail construction. Since it's a forgone conclusion that some water will find its way inside from time to time, you might as well drill several small holes in the box bottom to allow for drainage. Attach the top with inside hinges and allow an inch of overhang to help prevent water from running inside. Be sure to position the boxes where they will not interfere with fish fighting, anchoring or other everyday endeavors.

If you do a lot of live bait fishing for fluke, blues, sea trout, bass or other predators, a live-well becomes a necessity no matter what size your boat. Many manufacturers today offer live-wells as an option and if that's the case, opt for the largest well that will reasonably fit on your craft. The bigger the well, the more bait it will hold and the longer that bait will likely stay alive. Rounded wells seem to keep large, live bait in better shape than square or rectangular wells as the lack of corners equates to more swimming room for your "soon to be dinner" baitfish.

If your boat didn't come with a live well, you'll probably end up building your own. A simple one can be made using two large plastic trash cans, one slightly bigger than the other. Punch the smaller of the two cans full of one-half-inch diameter holes, keeping all the holes at least six inches from the can's bottom, and drop it into the larger container. Now fill the pails with sea water and add the live bait. When the bait begins to show signs of oxygen depletion, the inner can is lifted and allowed to drain into the outer one. The big can is then emptied over the side and refilled. Water changes must be frequent with this setup, though, and honestly I have grown too lazy to use this method any longer.

A better idea is to convert a 60 to 120 quart cooler into a bait tank. This takes less work than you might think -- certainly less work than emptying a large trash can full of water ten or twelve times each trip throughout the summer and fall. Simply place a bilge pump at the bottom of the cooler and attach a two or three foot length of flexible tube to the flush pipe. Run the tube from the pump, up one of the cooler's back corners and across the back of the cooler box just below the lid. Plug the tube with a water proof, glue-coated wooden dowel (or secure the dowel with a clamp or pair of small screws) and drill a series of small holes one half-inch apart along the length of the tube that runs horizontally below the cooler top. This creates a closed loop in which the bilge pump circulates water inside the cooler, spraying it out the hose so that it mixes with oxygen and thus aerates the tank. With this method, you shouldn't have to change any water at all unless it becomes bloody from an injured baitfish.

Speaking of coolers, you're going to need one to keep the day's catch unspoiled. After all, what's the sense of fishing if you can't bring home a good tasting dinner at least once in a while? Fish that are left to bake in a pailful of water or, worse, left on the deck, just don't retain that seaside freshness which fishermen relish on the dinner plate. Fish iced down in a cooler immediately after being caught usually do.

Like most other marine items, fishing coolers have come a long way in recent years and sturdy, efficient models are currently available in sizes ranging from 48 to 172 quarts, possibly larger. As with bait wells, those in the 60 to 120 quart range will do for most inshore situations, being both manageable and large enough to hold a good day's catch. Anglers who take home large bluefish or stripers may need to go all the way to the top end of the scale, possibly needing two of the largest models on some trips when filling the freezer is the prime objective.

Whether a cooler is chosen to serve as a stow-away box, live well or fish box, you're going to need a quality product that can take a beating. To that end, the following checkpoints should help you decide on a model that can stand up to the job. First, any cooler that is going to see boat use should have a drain plug at its base, preferably at one of the narrow ends. This will allow you to easily drain water off when necessary. No plug, no good. Second, look to see that the manufacturer lists "heavy duty foam insulation" as a feature of the cooler you are considering. This is often a sign of product quality which a surprising number of competitive coolers lack. Next, pick up the cooler and examine it closely. Does it look and feel sturdy? It better, for it's going to absorb a pounding some days when its filled with water, ice or fish and choppy seas mean a bumpy ride home. Can it serve as a seat for a child or adult? Are the handles advertised as unbreakable? A 172 quart cooler filled with codfish may weigh as much as 250 lbs. -- that can put a lot of strain where the handles are attached. Coolers for fishermen should also feature a removable food tray which will keep lunch or bait separate from the catch, though this option isn't important if you plan to use the cooler as a live well. Finally, check the latch. When closed, it should seal the cooler air tight. If it doesn't, cool air may be able to escape from the cooler, or worse, water may be able to enter. Both scenarios are unacceptable.

If you plan on fishing after dark, prime time for inshore predators like sea trout, weakfish, striped bass and bluefish, you'll need a flash or spotlight to aid in landing big fish, tying rigs, finding the bulkhead, chasing crabs on the surface, etc. These can be powerful setups requiring

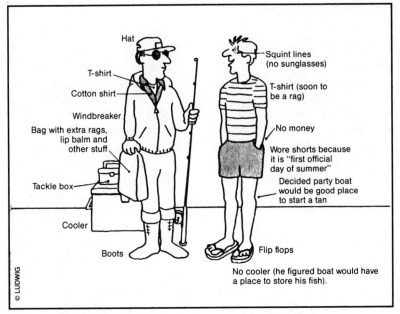

The Prepared Vs. The Unprepared Angler—Summer

hook-up to your main battery or more likely, small disposable or rechargeable flashlights which, with the addition of an elastic strap, can be hung around the neck in the fashion popularized by surfcasters.

Evening and nighttime fishing also means cruising with the running lights on. The U.S. Coast Guard requires running lights to be displayed by all boats that operate at night and most new craft come with these already in place. For vessels measuring less than 26 feet, one white light must be visible 360 degrees for a minimum of two miles. Additionally, one red port light and one green starboard light must be positioned so that oncoming boaters can see them from straight ahead to 112.5 degrees on either side.

Every boat needs an anchor, but which style will fit your needs the best? The answer may be to keep more than one kind on board if you fish in varied waters. Just think of the different bottom types worked by flounder, striped bass and tautog fishermen. In brief, the kind of anchor one needs is dictated by the size of the boat and the kind of bottom where fishing will be done. For securing over rocky bottoms or mussel beds, the traditional kedge style anchor (sometimes called "hook anchor") is the best bet. Anchoring in thick mud is a task better suited to a mushroom anchor, which is also ideal for slowing down a drift over any kind of bottom. The anchor that comes standard with most small and medium sized boats is called a danforth. This is the anchor with two large flukes designed to quickly dig in and hold over sandy bottoms (danforths and their anchor line, by the way, should always be separated by seven to ten feet of heavy chain as these anchors tend to plane and need just a little help to stay down on the bottom where the flukes can catch and dig in). For really rocky or obstructed bottoms, a cinder block might be the best choice as it can be sacrificed should it hang up in a wreck, cable, rockpile or other bottom debris.

Most small and medium sized boats have little trouble holding in quiet waters, but fishermen often anchor in strong currents along channel edges, river or harbor mouths, or inlets. In these areas, standard sized anchors don't always cut the mustard. Thus, it's a good idea to choose an anchor that's a bit on the heavy side for your boat. This will mean a little extra sweat when hauling it up, but it will also mean that your craft will stay put once the anchor grabs hold. For boats less than 16

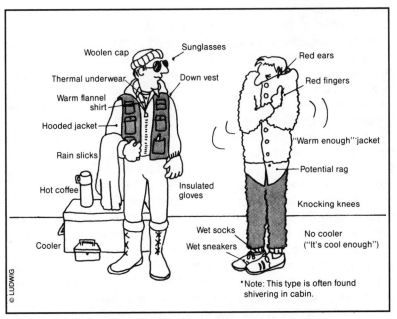

The Prepared Vs. The Unprepared Angler—Winter

feet, a five-pound anchor will usually suffice. Seagoing craft of 17 to 23 feet will find 10 to 20 pound weights a better choice.

When buying an anchor, don't skimp on the line. A good anchor line will last several years while a poor choice may not make it through the season. In general, nylon ropes are better than polypropylene for this task as the tendency of the latter to chafe can be quite rough on the hands. For anchoring in slow or moderate currents, you'll need about triple the water depth in line scope. Stronger currents dictate six or seven times the water depth.

I don't know that a compass should be called an accessory as it is truly a required instrument of navigation for any captain who travels out of sight of his moorings. Accessory or necessity, the compass is a great aid in fog or during nighttime sojourns when the lights of your own dock blend into the horizon along with what seems to be every other shorebound twinkle visible for six miles. If you intend on becoming a serious boater, buy a compass and learn to use it. To make things easier, keep handy a chart of readings to and from your usual destinations. It might save you from doing a lot of needless circling and possibly running aground.

There was a time, only a few years back, when computerized electronic navigational and fish-finding equipment was cost prohibitive for most of us. That time is now past. As much as some old fashioned diehards would like you to believe otherwise, fishing electronics are here to stay and they are becoming less costly while offering more and better features each and every month. In fact, at today's prices it's possible to purchase an LCD (Liquid Crystal Display) or LCR (Liquid Crystal Recorder) which can give readouts of Loran coordinates, water temperature, boat speed, and water depth, as well as mark fish, for $350 to $500 -- less than some Loran units alone would have cost five years ago! Loran, by the way, is a navigation system which uses land based radio signals to allow boaters to pinpoint their exact location while anywhere on the water. The availability of such low cost units have made fishing wizards out of virtual novices who, with the aid of "a good set of numbers" provided by a friend, chart or local fishing magazine, can locate wrecks and other hotspots with ease.

Personally, I like the romanticism of finding the fish on my own, but locating new wrecks, mussel beds, forgotten channels and the like by accident or even careful observation of surface currents and water color takes too long. On their days off most anglers want to fish, not explore. With some units now even possessing a degree of "user friendliness",

Many LCR's offer more than a simple representation of the bottom. This unit, for instance, provides a readout of surface water temperature, distance traveled from port and depth, in addition to marking fish. Some LCR's also double as Loran units.

even the most highly skilled fisherman must admit that it just doesn't make sense to do without these magic boxes.

Aside from cost, the main problem with any modern electronic or computerized aid is how quickly it becomes outdated. Whatever VHF-radios, recorders or other electronics you purchase now will be available with more power and better features next season. Don't let that discourage you from modernizing. That unit you purchase now will still be able to accomplish those jobs for which it was intended, even if later models can do more.

Which electronics should your boat have? That depends primarily on where you fish. While blue water adventurers will find a VHF-radio and Loran to be necessities, those who stay within sight of land usually will need nothing more than an LCR -- though the other niceties can be helpful. A radio, for instance, can allow one to eavesdrop on party or charter boat skippers, or communicate with another angler who may be over fish. The last instance, of course, works best between partners as anglers hot and heavy into action usually *don't* want to alert the fleet.

With electronic technology and terminology an ever changing blur right now, the best way to learn of the capabilities offered by this equipment is to take a trip to a reputable dealer or check out a working model on a friend's boat. Any feature covered here might very well change before you made a purchase so you'll just have to do a little homework. You should know, though, that the power of the unit and size of the monitor (display) have more effect on price than do small but pleasing features such as temperature gauges. Note, too, that LCD's and LCR's should always be installed so that the sun will not shine directly on the monitor screen. Just like any other computer screen, these displays are subject to "washout", a term used to describe the difficulty one has in seeing computer images through the sun's glare. Although glare screens are available for most displays, they are of minimal help when on the water.

Portable recorders and LCD's are more affordable now than ever before. They can help you locate productive underwater structure, deep holes and channel edges.

There are other accessories that come to mind when outfitting a boat for fishing. Boat poles, for example, come in handy around docks and moorings or when tying up to another craft while on the water. And motor extension handles, chum buckets, down riggers and anchor winches all serve their respective purposes. The list could go on and on. My advice regarding any of these other accessories is simple: Before purchasing, building or installing a new item, take a little time to shop around and ask other boat owners about their experiences with the various brand names. Dockside advice runs cheap for boaters; sometimes it's an overlooked bargain.

Chapter 3

⚓

General Thoughts On Tackle

For many anglers, selection of tackle is a hazy area. There are just so many choices, how could anyone know all there is to know about fishing tackle? Perhaps the best way to begin separating the hype and advertising from the functional facts is to fully understand the needs of a few basic setups. From there, one can always inquire about the added features.

Anglers and tackle manufacturers tend to classify rods and reels by their relative sturdiness, giving rise to the modern day concept of "light", "medium" and "heavy" tackle. Whether of spinning or conventional design, rods and reels must be viewed not so much in terms of the size or strength of their components as in their relationship to the fighting qualities of the species sought and the conditions under which fishing will be done. The same rod and reel combo which might be considered a "heavy" setup for bay fluke fishing for instance, might also be used as a "lightweight" setup for roving blues. The "lightweight" fluke pole, on the other hand, may well double as a meat stick for winter flounder or bay porgies. I think you get the picture; there is a lot of ambiguity in the classification of fishing tackle and, on the water, rod and reel combos frequently cross over from one category to another as the potential quarry changes.

With crossover possibilities specifically in mind -- after all, buying a separate outfit for each type of fish would be unreasonable, not to mention expensive -- most anglers will find that three basic setups can be used to cover the vast majority of inshore, salt water angling situations. These can be broken down into categories of bay, inlet or light ocean, and deep sea fishing setups.

To cover such species as bay porgies, fluke and flounder, as well as other fish which inhabit shallow or estuarine environments, a medium action bay setup is the best choice. This rig, ideally used in water depths of less than 20 feet, should be able to handle moderate tides and sinker weights of one to four ounces.

Typically, today's shallow water outfits consist of light to medium weight spinning or bait casting gear with the first probably outnumbering the latter on most small boats. The major advantages of spinning tackle are twofold: it allows for quick and easy casting and is relatively tangle free. Baitcasting or conventional outfits on the other hand offer greater line control, increased sensitivity and a bit more backbone, but also take an "educated thumb" to work properly -- even on those setups sporting anti-backlash braking. Either will suffice provided current strength isn't overbearing, but as currents increase in speed or water depth begins to exceed about twelve feet, the edge most decidedly shifts toward the more traditional gear.

For the spin fisherman, the ideal bay outfit will fall along the lines of a six to seven foot medium tapered rod and a quality, name brand reel designed to handle eight to twelve pound test lines. An adequate baitcasting or conventional selection would include a reel able to work lines testing 10 to 15 lbs. and a complementing five and a half to six and a half foot medium tapered rod. In either case, these setups need not be expensive, merely functional with smooth working drag systems.

The closer you look at it, the more you'll discover that there really is a lot of leeway when choosing outfits for shallow water fishing. In situations where casting range is discounted, baitcasting and spinning gear are almost interchangeable for bay flounder, fluke, sea trout and the like. In fact in many instances, one can get away with using a freshwater bass outfit and six or eight pound test line. Some anglers, myself included, actually prefer such "sweet water" setups when working in mild tempered depths of six feet or less.

Deeper waters and faster currents call for stronger measures. Therefore, those who ply their luck in inlets, fast moving channels, shallow ocean waters or pretty much any depth between twenty and sixty feet, will likely require a medium class conventional outfit or fairly heavy spinning gear. While conventional and spinning tackle may be interchangeable in bay-like scenarios, the choice for those working deeper and more turbulent waters is fairly clear cut. For the bottom fisherman, conventional gear makes more sense while those casting plugs and poppers for surface and mid-depth feeding stripers or blues will probably still prefer the luxurious ease and range of casting afforded by spinfishing.

Obviously, the fish which frequent ocean and inlet waters tend to be larger and more powerful than those found inside the bays. For this reason it is imperative that you select an outfit that is sturdy enough to dictate policy to any panicked fish. While rods of tree trunk proportions are not warranted, an adequate conventional setup will incorporate a strong but sensitive pole of five and a half to six and a half feet, matching 2/0 or 3/0 reel, and line testing 12 to 20 lbs. Such a setup will perform well with sinker weights between three and six ounces while hauling tough, straight up and down fighters like blackfish and seabass away from structure and potential snags. Those with reason for working spinning gear will find a seven foot rod, possessed of decent backbone and matched to a reel that can spool a large quantity of 12 to 20 lb. test

Tackle selections for the inshore angler should include a combination of spinning and conventional gear like that shown above. From right to left: ultra-light spinning, light conventional, medium-light spinning, medium baitcasting, heavy and extra heavy conventional setups.

line, should be up to the challenge. With the bigger fish likely to be found in the rougher waters, a smooth drag system takes on added importance and should be a prime consideration when selecting either setup.

Those persons who travel offshore seeking codfish, pollack, large bluefish, or other deepwater species, or who live line big baits aimed at tempting big bass and bluefish, will need stiffer medicine. Under these conditions, a rig able to control 30 to 40 lb. test lines and 8 to 16 oz. of lead should spearhead your arsenal. The reel selected for this kind of action should be a quality 3/0 or 4/0, dependable and rugged, with a retrieve ratio of at least 4:1. A high speed ratio is required because lines must often be reeled up from depths of 150 feet or more when deep sea fishing and, even in shallow water, slack must be taken up in a hurry when a trophy sized gamester speeds directly toward the angler. Furthermore, this outfit must also be capable of breaking from the bottom a fish that may weigh over 50 lbs., and have the guts to bring it to the surface in a reasonable amount of time. A "power" or extended handle will aid in cranking strong fish toward the boat and is especially helpful in areas where a green fish must be quickly decked to prevent compromising one's safety near bridge abutments, boulders, jetty rocks or ocean breakers.

While the tackle described above will see you through most fishing situations, there are times when more specialized gear comes into play. Setups designed for trolling, ultra-light and fly fishing are common examples. All three are somewhat limited in their applications, yet any one can be the ticket to success under given circumstances. Of the three, trolling gear sees the most action.

Actually, under some conditions any of the basic setups previously described can be used for trolling. Some back bay bassers and weakfish fanciers will, for instance, use light or medium weight spinning gear to drag whole sandworms and willow-leaf spinners between boulders and across shallow flats. Similarly, a small plug or tube lure can be affixed to the end of almost any line and trolled for cocktail blues feeding at an inlet mouth. Specialized trolling gear, however, is made to present baits or lures at predetermined depths, usually those which cannot be efficiently maintained by other tackle. Most trolling setups are also crafted to fill the cooler at the expense of sport.

For shallow water trolling where wire lines aren't necessary, the same rods and reels used for inlet or deep sea fishing should suffice. A 3/0 reel and 15 to 30 lb. test monofilament rates as the perfect match most of the time. Lighter gear, including spinning outfits, can also be put to use with the aid of downriggers. These are standard fare in the Great Lakes region but haven't really caught on in our local salt waters as yet. Essentially, a downrigger is little more than a heavy ball or drail attached via heavy (usually 60 to 100 lb. test) fishing line to a winch or crank. The angler connects his line to the ball via a small clip, allowing for several feet of space between the ball and lure. The ball is then lowered to an appropriate depth, and the lure follows along. A strike from a fish releases the angler's line from the clip, allowing the fish to be played without any added weight. In this way, it's possible to troll big fish on small lures with relatively light spinning or conventional gear.

In areas where fish regularly school deeper than fifteen or twenty feet, most salt water anglers prefer wire line setups. Standard fare for this route includes sturdy rods measuring six and a half to seven feet and 3/0 or 4/0 conventional style reels loaded with 40 lb. to 60 lb. test wire. The rods you select for wire line trolling should sport carbide or silicon/carbide guides as this kind of line will quickly groove just about anything else.

The reason straight monofilament setups can't compete with downriggers or wire line rigs when trolling deep has to do with the way these lines behave in the water. Although a lure or weight attached to the end of a mono line will sink as it pays out behind the boat, letting out more than fifty feet or so causes an arc to form in the line, planing your lures back toward the surface. Thus by the time an angler has let out 300 feet of mono in the hopes of reaching 30 foot depths, the end of the line with your lure attached is actually riding just below the waves! Wire line, conversely, sinks at a more consistent rate, approximately one foot for every ten feet of wire you let out. Thus, at 200 feet, your lures should be running 20 feet deep, at 250 feet, lure depth is 25 feet, and so on. Most anglers mark their wire line at 50 foot intervals (starting at 100 feet) with dental floss or shrink-wrap tape. You might even go a step further and color code your markings. This makes it easy to figure out how much line is in the water at any given time. Moving from marker to marker equates to about a five foot change in depth for the lure.

There are two kinds of wire lines commonly used today: stainless steel and monel. Although the stainless variety can be exceptionally strong, it kinks too easily, frequently negating the strength factor. For this reason, many charter captains and frequent trollers prefer the monel. In either case, make it a point to spool 100 yards or so of 50 lb. dacron backing on your reel. This will take up room on the spool, reducing the amount of wire line you'll require (it is expensive) while also preventing the wire from cutting or warping your reel spool. Backing may also serve to cushion the run of a big fish, reducing stress as line peels out against the drag.

While trolling setups are often made to "hoist 'em in", ultra-light tackle dangles the carrots of challenge and glory ahead of the sporting angler, promising thrills and fast hook-ups while realistically offering only a fair chance of whipping a decent sized fish. Still, any hook-up is good while it lasts and the satisfaction garnered by beating the odds is considered by some to be unparalleled.

For the inshore salt water angler, ultra-light tackle is generally considered to revolve around lines testing two to four pounds. These are usually but not always spooled on miniscule spinning reels paired with wispy five to five and a half foot rods. The lighter you go with one of these setups, the more the odds tilt in favor of the quarry; or as ultra-light enthusiasts prefer to think of it, the greater the challenge. Unfortunately, even medium-sized salt water predators overpower these setups and it often takes a dozen hookups or more to land one large fluke, bluefish or striper. There may be a better success ratio on the horizon, however. Over the last few years, some freshwater salmon and steelhead anglers have greatly increased their ultra-light success by teaming tiny spinning reels with "noodle rods" -- very fast tapered, light action nine to twelve footers that to me seem more like extended fly rods than anything else. These rods are designed to really absorb the pulsing, surging struggles of large fighting fish, cushioning line shock and reducing the incidence of breakoffs. As a rule of thumb, these anglers use longer rods for lighter lines. I don't see why that wouldn't work in the briny -- though I imagine it would be quite interesting to watch someone single handedly attempt to net a big blue at the end of a 12 foot rod while remaining seated in a small tin boat. Still, if ultra-light fun is your cup of tea, these rods might well be worth a shot.

In general, ultra-light tackle is at its best when working single, small lures just below the surface. Casting three-inch plugs for mackerel or cocktail blues can be a blast at times, and larger but not overly powerful predators like sea trout and weakfish offer a reasonable expectation of success; even trophy sized fish can be bested by the skillful. Working

Some species, weakfish and sea trout included, are especially susceptible to a well presented shrimp immitation or snazzy streamer fly.

ultra-light tackle for big chopper blues, however, can be an exercise in frustration unless trying for a line class record is the day's objective.

Speaking of records: Although ultra-light lines are difficult to control in rough water or windy weather, it should be noted that in the hands of a cagey veteran, they are capable of defeating some pretty big gamefish. A look at the current I.G.F.A. two and four pound line class records will quickly prove this fact, as the lead entries for several popular species range between 10 and 20 lbs. If you want to get your name in the record books, this is one way to do it. Many salt water line class records are still open and others are quite vulnerable.

The popularity of salt water fly fishing has grown dramatically in recent years; most often it is practiced on the smaller inshore species discussed in this book. While there isn't room for an in-depth discussion here, a few words can be said.

I've done some inshore fly casting and have found it quite rewarding. I own a nine foot, two-piece, medium weight fly rod and single action reel filled with an eight-weight, weight forward, floating line. I don't use it much unless weakfish, blues, stripers or mackerel are on the surface, but when I take it out, it sure sees a lot of fun. Although I've never taken a fish over 12 lbs. with this setup, it is perfect for chasing school sized back-bay predators when the wind lies down enough to make casting easy. Sometimes when gamefish are feeding mainly on shrimp or very small livebait, or on nights when the water is filled with "fire", a flyrod and three-inch streamer, tiny popper or small shrimp imitation is the quickest way to score. You might want to give it a shot with a similar setup, just to see if you find this kind of action stimulating enough to further pursue. Chances are you will.

While learning how to properly use different kinds of tackle may take a little time, newcomers seem to quickly realize that the rods and reels used by expert anglers are often expensive, customized outfits, personalized in design and sometimes costing well over a hundred dollars. In the hands of a highly knowledgeable angler, such tools work like magic to tame even the largest of gamefish. For the novice, however, name brand items can usually perform the same tasks and though offering fewer features than the high-end gear, are usually more tolerant of human error. Thus, it may not be a good idea to run out looking for top of the line outfits until you've learned enough to know precisely what you need and want. If that means taking some time to experiment with different kinds of tackle, so be it. The more you fish and try new equipment, the more you'll begin to get a feel for the tackle styles that best suit your particular brand of fishing.

No matter how good or expensive the rods and reels you own may be, they'll be of little help in procuring fillets if the line that goes with them isn't fit for duty. While line choice is important to any angler it takes on added importance in a salt water environ where heavy weights, big baits or lures, powerful gamefish and shellfish beds, wrecks, rock bottom or other structure all combine to take their toll. In the rough and tumble world of coastal angling, lines of dubious quality don't stand a chance.

Although monofilament lines are almost always used on light tackle and still predominate even when the heavy gear is taken out, many experienced fishermen prefer dacron or braided nylon when using lines in the 36 lb. class or heavier. These lines stretch less than does the mono, making for reduced "bellying" and easier hookups in deep or fast moving waters. The obvious drawback to these lines is their high visibility. They are also less forgiving of angler mistakes due to their lack of stretch (especially dacron). While dacron or braided nylon is a good choice for the expert, beginners will probably benefit a little more from the forgiving qualities of a brand name monofilament. Look for "abrasion resistant" lines whenever possible.

Slice it any way you want, there can be no denying that fishing tackle gets to be expensive. Fortunately, most of the items offered by the big name vendors are built to last provided they receive a modicum of care and preventive maintenance. I have several setups, in fact, that have seen six to eight years of action with little more than a good greasing and change of drag washers required to keep them going. To ensure that new combo you've just purchased sees more than a season or two of service, it is vital that you give it a good cleaning after each trip. Salt is a very corrosive mineral and believe me, it will find its way into every nook and cranny of your reel as well as coat your rod by the end of each trip. If left on a reel, salt will slowly eat away at the gears rendering your tackle useless in a matter of months. It can also do quite a number on rod guides. Take a few minutes to keep your tackle fit by washing it down with warm, soapy water after each trip (a toothbrush works well for getting sand and grit out of hard to reach areas). You should also oil the drag mechanism and check all parts the manufacturer recommends attending to. Change the line whenever it appears to be weakening or by mid-season even if it appears to be in top condition. Taking care of your tackle will help ensure that all is in proper working order, cutting down the number of unpleasant surprises than can pop up after you've set the hook on a good fish

If after reading this chapter you still have trouble deciding on what tackle to use, or would simply like to gather additional information, stop by your local tackle shop and ask some questions. The people there should be able to help.

It's time now for a few words on clothing and other supplies. From a fishing standpoint, it's always better to have too much than too little clothing. A jacket or sweater can be removed as temperatures become uncomfortably hot, but unless it has been brought along clothing simply cannot be added when cool breezes begin to blow.

Balanced baitcasting or spinning gear is ideal for tossing small plugs and jigs to shallow feeding predators like these two to three pound cocktail blues.

Just to be on the safe side, always plan to deal with the most adverse weather conditions that might arise while you will be on the water. When packing for your fishing trip, remember that meteorologists are frequently off base with their weather forecasts. Also remember that temperatures on the water, especially offshore, can run 10 to 20 degrees cooler than on dry land. Thus, a sunny, shirt sleeve, 68 degree day in your backyard is possibly a brisk, 53 degree sweater day over ocean or bay waters.

No matter how pleasant the weather, always make it a point to pack along at least one extra sweater or hooded sweatshirt and a pair of long pants per person, just in case a chill develops. It's also advisable to wear a light, waterproof windbreaker as protection against cool breezes. The summertime fisherman will be able to get away with a sweater or jacket, a cap or sunglasses to reduce glare, and a bottle of sun screen lotion. During the winter season, however, a knit wool hat, scarf, thermal underwear and rubber insulated gloves become necessary items. Dress with several layers of clothing during winter outings rather than one heavy, bulky coat. Quite a few studies have demonstrated that layers of clothing conserve heat much more efficiently than do large, bulky jackets and, as mentioned before, clothing can always be removed if it gets hot out. Dressing in layers will allow you to peel off a piece or two of clothing until you feel comfortable, whereas one bulky coat might leave you with the choice of being a little too hot or a little too cold.

You can, of course, consider topping off several layers of clothing with a bulky coat or jacket for those cold winter outings.

Spring and fall are the seasons when most anglers are caught unprepared. The weather at these times of year can be quite turbulent and unpredictable. Many a spring and fall day have I stood at the stern and froze my buns off because I believed predictions of 70 degree temperatures. Anyone has enough sense to dress warmly during the months of December, January and February, but many people who should know better get left out in the cold during March, April, September, October and November.

Although specialized clothing is not essential to fishing success, a good set of rain slicks or foul weather gear and water resistant boots will keep you cleaner and dryer. Many fishermen wear only the overalls and boots, leaving the jacket aside unless it gets cold out or begins to rain. The beauty of foul weather gear is not only that you stay dry, but that at day's end your clothing will not smell fishy or be stained from bait and catch. The boots, aside from keeping your little toes toasty and dry, will help prevent the loss of footing on slippery decks. They also prevent your favorite pair of running shoes from smelling like fish bait, chum and bilge water. Real fishermen, by the way, wear their boots even when they don summertime shorts -- style be damned.

Aside from clothing, there are several other items which will help make the fishing day pass more smoothly. First and foremost among these are rags. I wish I had a fish for every time I've seen an angler scour the boat in search of a stray cloth with which to wipe his hands. I'd be able to open my own fish market. Always make it a point to throw a few rags in the bucket before leaving home or, better yet, stash a plastic trash bag full of rags on board at the start of the season. This will ensure that you never have to go without. Torn undershirts or old towels make great boat rags.

Lunch is another item to be considered. You will get very hungry on the water, and if you don't bring along a good lunch you will likely regret it! Although many anglers plan on running back to the dock for a short trip to the deli, this idea is quickly scrapped once the fish begin to bite. To be on the smart side, bring along several sandwiches or a large hero and a six pack of your favorite beverage. When packing your lunch, be sure to shy away from dressings such as mayonnaise or food that will turn bad if exposed to warm temperatures. Even if they're in the cooler much of the time, these items could spoil during a long day on the water.

If you are on any type of medication, remember to bring it with you. Again, no one likes to return to the dock after casting off and unless you are in dire need your fishing buddies are likely to consider such a retreat a serious inconvenience. Even if you are scheduled to take your medicine after returning to port, it's a good idea to bring along all you might need just in case you get back late.

Of course, you'll require some type of bag to carry on extra clothes and miscellaneous items. Most of this can be stored in a waterproof carry-all or duffle bag. Large plastic trash bags work OK too, as long as you are not transporting anything heavy. Some anglers use 5 gallon pails and these work very well. If possible, choose one with a secure, snap-on lid. This will hold a good deal of tackle if you don't use a tackle box and in a pinch can serve as an extra seat (if turned upside down) or as a container to hold your catch.

A very important topic for the small boat angler is coolers or other vessels for storing fish on the boat and later in the car on the trip home. Since this subject was covered thoroughly in Chapter 2, we won't discuss it here.

The following is a checklist of items which may be helpful on any fishing trip. Not all are necessities but each one will prove useful at one time or another.

FISHING CHECKLIST
CLOTHING
1. Windbreaker or jacket
2. Sweatshirt or sweater
3. Long pants
4. Hat or sunglasses
5. Rain slicks or other foul weather gear
6. Boots

For winter add:
1. Thermal socks and underwear
2. Sweaters and/or hooded sweatshirts (at least two)
3. Insulated gloves
4. Knit hat
5. Scarf

TACKLE
1. Rod and reel combos (spare spools) to cover anticipated possibilities
2. Spare weights, rigs and lures
3. Long nose cutting pliers
4. Knife
5. Rags
6. Bucket, cooler or burlap sack to store your catch
7. Net or gaff
8. Fish scale

MISCELLANEOUS
1. Bait and chum
2. Lip balm
3. Small first aid kit
4. Medication as needed (as for diabetes, heart condition, etc.)
5. Sun screen or sun block lotion
6. Lunch, including beverages
7. Camera and film
8. Binoculars
9. Lubricant for reel
10. Seasickness medication
11. Wallet or money
12. Fish tags
13. Extra can or two of outboard motor oil

For winter add:
1. Thermos of hot cocoa, coffee, or tea

Chapter 4

⚓

Fitting In:
Safety Rules And The
Unwritten Codes

The small rental boat looked out of place as it sputtered over a heavy swell and settled in alongside several larger craft drifting near the inlet mouth. The ebbing tide was retreating at full tilt as it had been for almost an hour, spilling a confused cargo of struggling baitfish out into the ocean depths. Though it was a mild day weather-wise, navigation was a bit difficult due to the powerful current and a strong rip which marked the area where shoaling had formed an east/west sandbar. Over the past two seasons the bar had grown to the point that it now nearly severed the main channel in two. At least one captain warned the driver of the tiny skiff that his boat was too small to be working such turbulent waters and that, in any case, the entire inlet was off limits to the rentals per the livery's posted rules. The advice, though, went unheeded, and that nearly proved to be a fatal mistake.

Both blues and fluke were hitting hard that morning, just ahead of the rip and sometimes right at its edge. Getting in on the action required a seventy-five yard drift with the engine running, and the wisdom to pull up and bear east in order to skirt the shoal's inshore edge without getting caught in the turbulence. From there one could circle back uptide to again take a place in what by unspoken consent had become a well defined drift lane.

On its first float through the area, the small boat was cautious, coming within only fifty yards or so of the rip. I watched as what I presumed to be a grandfather, father and son combined to take three fat fluke, one about three pounds. Then, anxious to get back over the place where they had first hooked up, the skiff's captain turned the craft in a tight circle and zig-zaged between the larger, drifting boats, dodging the fury of a following sea until cutting into the line about half way back to the unofficial starting point. The rental's course caused at least one skipper to maneuver out of the way and call out something I couldn't quite decipher.

The second drift for the skiff appeared to be less productive -- at least I didn't witness anything come up on that pass. This time the boat came within about 20 yards of the rip before peeling off and heading back in the same manner as before. It was now clear that although the little boat was having difficulty negotiating the rolling waves that preceded the choppy rip waters proper, the anglers on board were not going to be intimidated by the forces of nature.

I was working a good blue well ahead of the white-capped turbulence as the skiff drifted past for a third try. Having my hands full with eight pounds of fun, I didn't really look over again until the battle had been won. When I finally did turn around, the skiff and its passengers had vanished. I felt that queasy, sinking feeling in my stomach as I scanned the rip intently. The feeling seemed to be intensified by the fact I never heard a scream or sound of panic -- perhaps with the pounding surf in the background and the noise generated by my own engine, plus the roar of the rip, any calls for help had been drowned out. It took about three seconds to spot the bobbing, upturned hull. It was rapidly being sucked out to sea and across the shoal by the boiling tide, three generations of anglers (sans life preservers) in tow broadside to the punishing waves.

There was little anyone could do to help but race around to the tail end of the rip and hope the unlucky fishermen could hold on, which they did. While the boat was eventually uprighted and towed back to shore, tackle, cameras and other possessions were lost forever, and three very embarassed and humbled gentlemen had to be plucked from the water by the same captain who had earlier offered fair warning. Worse yet, wet and cold the sorry trio had to return to the dock to face what must have been one mighty sore livery master.

Not only had these anglers bit off more than they could chew, they had violated Coast Guard advice, boat livery guidelines, and several laws of common sense. In the process, they had greatly endangered their own lives and possibly the lives of their rescuers.

There is a lot more involved in skippering a boat than powering to the nearest hotspot and hauling in a hefty catch. Safety regulations and the rights of others enjoying their day on the high seas must also be considered. According to the U.S. Coast Guard, there are more than nine million motorboats using this country's waterways and that number is increasing every year. Add to this the growing popularity of jetskies and sail boating and you can imagine how busy the water becomes in any metropolitian or resort area. Of course not all boats are used for fishing, but as long as they are on the water, you will have to be aware of, deal with, and respect them.

As a boating captain, you are ultimately responsible for the safety of your passengers as well as for not endangering those in other boats. The first responsibility can be dealt with through adherence to Coast Guard, state and local boating regulations, a knowledge of proper boating procedures and navigation, and an awareness of your immediate situation and the waters you're heading into. The second responsiblity often falls in place with compliance to the above, but it doesn't hurt to add a little courtesy and observence of what I like to call the "unwritten rules".

In terms of equipping your boat for safety's sake, you can start by carrying appropriate life preservers. There should be at least one USCG-approved personal floatation device (PFD) for each person onboard. PFD's come in a wide array of styles, a few of which are fairly comfortable. Although many anglers avoid doing so, PFD's of one kind of another should be worn at all times while on the water, especially in cold weather. Studies show that over 85% of all boating fatality victims were not wearing life preservers when misfortune suddenly struck. No matter how many PFD's you keep stowed away on board, they won't do any good unless you wear one or have time to put one on. As you can see from the story related above, some accidents happen too quickly to allow for the second option. In addition to PFD's worn by passengers, boats measuring 16 feet or more are also required to have ready at least one USCG-approved throwable PFD. For the small boater, this usually amounts to a bouyant seat cushion or life ring. It's really a good idea to have at least one throwable PFD on board any boat -- even those powered solely by oars and muscle power.

Fire extinguishers are not federally required on outboard motorboats of open construction which measure less than 16 feet and do not carry passengers for hire, but they should really be considered a necessity on any craft with a gas motor. All such engines have the potential to catch fire, and that includes small outboards. Get yourself a portable extinguisher and secure it to the hull or console where it will be easy to reach. Even if you never need to use it, you'll at least have the comfort of knowing it is close at hand.

A small first aid kit is another boating necessity and will come in handy more often than you might think. Such a kit should include, aside from the usual band aids and sterilizing solutions, a bottle of asperin, burn ointment and a small allotment of any special medication that you need to take daily (i.e., pills for diabetes or heart condition). You might also include some bee sting or insect bite relief. Tupperware containers make excellent storage boxes for your medical supplies.

Even if you only fish within sight of land, engine trouble could strand you for the better part of the day or even overnight. It's a wise skipper, then, who keeps a couple of cans of emergency drinking water and some non-perishable food stashed away on board. These need not be fancy, just enough to keep the crew from starting a mutiny should you be stuck for more than a few hours. With the thought of breakdowns fresh in mind, let me mention here that it is also a good idea to let someone know approximately where you intend to fish. That way if you miss curfew the Coast Guard will have an idea of where to begin searching.

Although engines occasionally break down on the water, many can be repaired on the spot, at least temporarily, provided there are a few basic tools and spare parts handy. A tool box armed with extra fuses, cotter pins, shear pins and spark plugs will prove a big relief at times. Include in your box a set of phillips and straight-edged screwdrivers, assorted wrenches, hammer, electrical tape, pliers, a pair of wire cutters and a few appropriately sized screws, bolts, nuts and wire caps. You might also keep on board somewhere an extra prop and several hand-held or parachute (red) flares. Keep any tools that are to be left on the boat well oiled, for dampness has a way of rusting or corroding just about any metal aid that isn't kept in an air and water tight container. In case the tools aren't enough to get the job done, you should also have a pair of oars tucked away somewhere on board.

Navigation in fog or after dark requires all of the above plus a horn or whistle on boats measuring 16 feet or more. After 1990, "a sound producing device" will be a federal requirement on motor boats of any type. Really, though, all boats that fish in such conditions should be so equipped. Nighttime cruising will also mandate use of running lights and a compass. Both of these items (plus flashlights) were discussed in Chapter 2.

Once you've got these basic safety items covered, you might want to invite a member of your local Coast Guard Auxiliary aboard for a Courtesy Marine Examination (CME). This is a free check of your boat and its equipment covering federal and state safety related requirements plus additional standards recommended by the Auxiliary. It is not a law enforcement activity and no report of you or your boat will be made to any agency as a result of the exam. If your boat passes the test, you will be issued a CME decal. If it dosen't pass, the inspecting officer will offer suggestions for improvement. To be awarded a decal, boats must prove seaworthy, meet predetermined safety standards, and possess some or all of the following according to boat size and classification: PFD's, fire extinguisher, sufficient ventilation, backfire flame arrester, visual distress signals, suitable portable fuel containers, adequate anchor and anchor line, alternate propulsion (i.e. oar or pole), and dewatering device (i.e. pump, bucket, scoop, etc.),

While most boaters are willing to take time setting up their craft as described above, it seems that not quite so many are eager to invest time learning the basic rules of navigation. This results in the chaos that often reigns whenever more than two boats try to use the same paths. Which craft has the right of way when vessels are on intersecting courses? Sometimes it seems that *nobody* knows the correct answer! Does one stay to the left or right of a particular kind of buoy? The wrong guess here could quickly put you aground. How do you deal with a heavy, following sea? Collision? Hypothermia? Gasoline fire? Knowing the right answers could possibly save your life. The Coast Guard Auxiliary offers several kinds of boating courses (some free) to answer these and other important questions that all boaters should consider before taking to the water. Take advantage of this service, especially if this is to be your first season as a skipper. You'll be amazed at how much less confusing boating and fishing can be with a little seafaring knowledge under your belt.

In addition to boating courses, the Coast Guard Auxiliary offers several short pamphlets which boaters may find helpful. For more information on these contact your local Coast Guard station, listed in the phone book under government agencies, or call this toll-free, boating information number: 1(800) 336-BOAT.

Most landlubbers manage to obey traffic signs while driving on solid ground, yet many boaters seem to miss the same kind of signs posted on the water. It should go without saying that posted restrictions such as speed limits, No Wake Area, Low Bridge, and Do Not Pass signs must command your immediate attention. Such warnings are displayed to ensure the safety of yourself and others who may be swimming, shellfishing, boating or enjoying various other kinds of coastal activity. Even when no one else is in sight, your craft's wake might prove destructive to moored boats, docks, etc., so think before you push down on the throttle. Rules of common sense, though rarely posted, should also cross one's mind before the dock lines are removed from their cleats. Take a minute before casting off to map out a strategy and scan the water ahead for debris or potential trouble of any kind. Be alert, stay out of water that appears overly rough, and study a chart of local waters so that you'll have a good idea as to the lay of main channels and water depths in any area you may have to cross. Keep a waterproof chart on board for quick and easy reference.

Bridging the gap between law and common sense is the topic of alcohol, the abuse of which while on the water is of growing concern in many areas these days. Each year, boating accidents kill about 1,000

U.S. citizens and seriously injure thousands more. Alcohol is a factor in roughly half the deaths. I'll not deny that some fishermen enjoy their spirits, but as with driving a car, the person at the helm should abstain. Boating takes a toll on the body, both physically and mentally. Even on a sunny day, bumpy rides, glare, wind and the concentration required to fish or get from point A to point B, not to mention an early start or late finish, all combine to wear you down. The use of alcohol accelerates the downward slide, quickly affecting judgement, balance, coordination, vision and reaction time. It's just as dangerous to operate a boat under the influence of alcohol (or drugs) as it is to drive a car in an unfit condition. It is also against the law in most states.

Two common miscues that can get even the most sober captain in serious trouble on the water are improper loading and unsafe anchoring technique. Both are responsible for the swamping or capsizing of many small craft each year.

In the case of loading small boats, it is vital that any amount of substantial weight be evenly distributed -- this includes your own weight and that of your passengers. Concentrating too much weight on one side or end of the boat will result in an awkward, clumsy ride. Usually, the boat will list toward the heavy side, allowing the quick movement of a person (or heavy item) toward the lean of the craft to simply roll it over. When added weight is evenly distributed, even a small skiff can support several passengers and a considerable amount of tackle. Still, it should be noted that just because a vessel stays afloat dosen't mean it isn't dangerously overloaded. Boats carrying too heavy a load, even when it is well spread out, behave sluggishly, plowing through rather than gliding across the water. In most instances, the bow rides high while the transom sits low with drastically reduced freeboard. One good wave rolling over a low transom from a following sea is often enough to swamp a boat in this handicapped position. Sometimes, a captain will realize his predicament and quickly stop to reposition some gear. The moment the boat slows, a wave from behind catches up to the stern and the real trouble begins.

Anchoring seems like it should be such an easy task, yet it too can lead to trouble if not done properly. The main rule here is simple to remember: Anchor only from the bow, even if you plan to double anchor. Anchoring from midship or the stern makes the boat more vulnerable to waves or wakes that could swell over the gunwale or transom. Imagine if you had double anchored from the stern and then moved up to the bow or amidship to fish. Now a rogue wave manages to top your transom, which was being held low in the water by the pressure of the current pushing against the rear of the boat. Your first reaction? Probably to dash to the back and let loose the anchor lines -- but wait! Moving to the back of the boat will sink the stern further, concentrating all the water in your craft right where you want it least! This may allow even a small wave to flood the boat from behind. Better be more careful. Perhaps using a gaff to grasp the anchor line behind the stern will allow you to loosen the tension a bit, or if you have a pair of oars tucked away on board rowing in reverse might help. Other than that, your're in quite a bind and had better start bailing even as you prey.

A second rule of anchoring, too often disregarded, is to keep the engine running in neutral until the anchor has fully set. This is especially so when working near jetty rocks, boulders, structure such as bulkheads or bridge abutments, or close to skinny water. Should the anchor fail to catch bottom for any reason, a running engine can be quickly placed in gear allowing the boat to maneuver away from potential hazards, reposition and try again. With the motor off, there might not be time enough to start up and take evasive action. On some boats, there isn't even a guarantee the motor will start on the first or second try.

Finally, remember to check the weather forecast before heading out and keep in mind the old taboo about standing up in small, unsteady boats. There seems little need to elaborate further on either of these points.

In addition to laws of safety and navigation, there is a set of unwritten rules shared between boating anglers that help give a sense of order to the fleet and keep misunderstandings to a minimum. Many of these codes in one way or another deal with allowing for a little space between boats and anglers, even when several craft are working a single school of fish. There is a kind of fictional force field which surrounds most fishing boats; a small area considered to be private domain by the anglers on board each craft. This area isn't fixed, rather it is flexible in size and constanlty adjusted to meet changing conditions and the entrance to or exit from the fishing scene by other boats. Further, it picks up and moves with each boat wherever that craft may head. In most instances, this space is just enough to prevent other boats from interfering with the playing of a hooked fish. Thus, this invisible shield often varies according to the characteristics of the species sought. Be

Children should don life preservers anytime they approach the water.

aware of the need for a little space between boats and remember not to crowd the shorebound caster either. Being more limited in the waters he can reach, it's likely his force field covers a little extra territory.

In the same basic vein of thought, let me draw your attention to the importance of fishing in a manner compatible with those around you. Anchoring in the line of a steady stream of drifting or trolling boats is taboo. So is trolling (or even driving) through someone else's well placed chumslick. If you are going to fish in a manner that might disrupt the prospecting of others, it's often best to move off and try your luck in a less busy area. If drifting or trolling with the fleet, simply get in line and take your turn over the best waters as space allows. Cutting off other boats in an attempt to monopolize the fish can result in a shower of unpleasantries.

At times when anchoring is the primary method, such as when working schools of winter flounder, sea trout, blackfish and seabass, be sure to position your boat so that it dosen't cut off the fish heading toward a neighbor's chum slick. Also, make sure not to block off the main channel to the point where cruising boats can't get through without slowing to a crawl.

There is one other unwritten rule that should be stressed here: Never race full throttle into a school of surface feeders. This action will usually put the fish down fast, raising the ire of anyone who was in good position before you blundered onto the scene. If you see fish working on top, slowly and quietly align your boat ahead of the action, leaving thirty or forty yards as a buffer zone. If you do it right, it will only take a minute or two before the fish have your boat surrounded. You can then join in the fun without causing any undue mayhem.

Of course, not all fishermen abide by such civil guidelines. Some anglers simply don't know any better and a few probably just don't care. The more anglers that make an effort to fit in, though, the easier and better the fishing will be for everyone.

Part II:
The Party Boat Game

Like a small, neighborhood game of poker, it doesn't take much of an ante to sit in on a hand of party boat fun. As in card games, however, strategy plays the leading role in a player's chances for success -- and it's hard to win big if you don't know the odds or understand the rules.

The following section details the strategies involved in choosing a productive boat from which to fish, selecting or renting the appropriate equipment, and outfitting yourself to stay warm, dry, and comfortable while on the water. It also covers the rules of etiquette which help make the game flow smoothly.

In short, this section is intended to tilt the odds in your favor so that you'll come out a winner at the party boat game!

Chapter 5

⚓

Welcome Aboard!

Why go party boat fishing at all? Aren't the boats too crowded? Don't they cost too much? These are about the commonest words of rebuke, often spoken by those privileged enough to own their own craft, or those who simply aren't comfortable unless they're casting from shore, pier, or surf. Yet this popular type of fishing needs no justification to those who have given it a try. It frequently offers advantages over any other kind of fishing -- and it is filled with personalities, intangibles and contradictions enough to make any day interesting. It's a whole different world on these craft, with an atmosphere that some find as addicting as fishing itself.

Certainly, from a practical point of view, party boat (AKA open boat, head boat) fishing makes a great deal of sense. To many without access to private or rented craft, party boating provides the only affordable means to reach productive locations that are beyond the reach of shoreline casting.

For a fair price the angler is ferried out to the fishing grounds in relative comfort. The task of locating the fish, as well as the worry of navigation, falls solely upon the shoulders of the captain and his electronic gear. Anchoring, chumming, netting or gaffing and in most cases, even such chores as cutting and distributing the bait, fall to the mates. In essence, all the fisherman need do is relax and fish knowing that all else has been taken care of. And party boaters do catch fish! Which, probably, is the best reason of all for joining the fun.

At the close of the day the angler need merely place his rod in its holder and enjoy the boat ride home. If one chooses, the mates can be asked to clean the catch (a small tip or fee is customary), making it possible to arrive at dockside with no more than tackle and a bag of clean fillets to bring home. What a bargain!

Even for those lucky enough to own or have access to private craft, party boating allows the chance to fish offshore grounds which are too far to reach in smaller boats. Additionally, if you figure in the cost of mooring or trailering, gas used while on the water, the purchase of chum and bait, plus the bodily pounding taken on a long ride in a small boat, the $25 to $35 price tag of most open boat trips begins to take on added appeal. Best of all, there's no scouring, hauling or cleaning the boat at the end of the day when you are simply too bushed to do what needs to be done.

If that's not enough, party boats can also transport and outfit an entire family in relative comfort -- an aspect considerably lacking in most private boats. With most open vessels today sporting a heated galley, cushioned chairs, hot snacks and men's and women's bathrooms, your family can relax inside the cabin, comfortably warm and without the bump, bump, bump, of a small and crowded boat slamming against a chop on the water. Need I mention the advantages of heated hand-rails, which are slowly becoming standard among the fleet, for early spring, late fall or winter excursions? For cold weather cod, blackfish, whiting, ling, flounder, bluefish and even mackerel fishing, it's hard to beat a party boat for comfort and results. In fact, between Labor Day and Memorial Day, even some of my diehard private boating friends will grudgingly admit that this is the best way to sail when the air is crisp.

Most party boats have tackle available for rent, usually two to five dollars for a rod, reel and complete rigging. Many even offer this as a free service. To the prospective fisherman who has not pursued a certain species because of lack of suitable equipment, this is a deal that's hard to pass up.

We've all had friends who call at 5:30 A.M. the morning of a trip to tell us that they can't possibly take the boat out as the lawn needs to be mowed. Other friends tell us we're welcome aboard anytime, but their free time and ours never coincides. Frustrating at times, isn't it? Weather permitting, most party boats sail every day, all season long. Some even sail right through the dead of winter. All you need do is arrive at the advertised sailing time and pay the fee. This regular schedule assures that there will always be a ship ready to take you to the fishing grounds, perhaps with a new found friend to share the day!

For the novice fisherman, whether child or adult, a party boat fishing trip can be a great learning experience. With helpful mates and plenty of experienced fishermen aboard, all one must do is ask for help and a friendly face should be found nearby, ready to offer plenty of free advice.

From knot tying to playing the fish, small clusters of anglers gather about the ship to compare notes. Should you feel uncomfortable seeking help from fellow fishermen, simply ask the mate. His job is to help you have a successful and fun day. A good mate will take pride in helping you to learn the ropes and improve your score. Even simply standing at the rail and keeping a watchful eye on other anglers will allow the observant fisherman to acquire new and pertinent information. For the private boater, in fact, a party boat trip is an excellent means of learning about unfamiliar species, finding hotspots or scouting new waters to which you can return again and again with your own craft. Always keep in mind that the amount of free information available on an open boat is considerable, even to the most experienced of anglers.

Are you prone to seasickness? Many sufferers of "mal du mer" find that the stability of a 60 to 180-foot ship under their feet prevents the occurrence of this tormenting disorientation. Those who are still affected tend to find the dizziness and vomiting to be much less severe than that experienced on smaller craft. For this reason alone, many anglers I know use their private boats for bay or inshore trips and turn to the head boats whenever a journey to offshore waters is required to get in on the action. If nothing else, at least those who do get sick can stand up, stretch their legs and take a walk around as they attempt to regain composure. (With today's medication, seasickness can often be greatly alleviated. For more information on seasickness prevention, see the sidebar in Chapter 18).

Last, but certainly not least among the practical reasons for party boating, is the fact that visitors from other cities or states (even countries) can shuffle aboard. This means that a freshwater bass enthusiast from the mid-west can visit the coast and fish for blues or other salt water species with all the help and information necessary for success at his finger tips -- and without the purchase of expensive new equipment. Best of all, if you're playing host you need not worry about outfitting a potential fumble fingers with your own cherished tackle! To look at it another way, one can visit any coastal state and give the local action there a go without inconveniencing those with whom he is staying. Fishing licenses, by the way, rarely if ever have to be purchased for a salt water party boat trip.

Based on practicality alone, then, open boat fishing is a decided bargain. But more than practical reasons draw people to the party boats. There's a certain aire about these vessels, a mystique if you will, peculiar to each ship. Each boat sails admidst the glory of its most productive days, while held strongly in the ghost-like presence of long forgotten "regulars". You can almost feel it when you step aboard. Yet despite the shroud of mystery, most party boats seem to greet you with a great big smile and open arms.

"Step right up! Plenty of blues. Big blues!" hawks the mate standing on the bow of a proud looking ship. "We slaughtered them yesterday!" Two slips further down the dock, a large orange and blue sign advertises "Porgy Time!" But it's not so much the shouts of the mate or the glare of the signs as it is the proud stance of the ship that finally draws you aboard.

Intangibles such as these make party boat fishing the great experience that it is. Friendships are struck up which may last a lifetime...or only till the end of the day. Each day a diversity of people from all walks of life, with varied character, background, and fishing experience, assemble on board to become comrades in fun for a few short hours. All guards are dropped, and men, women and children take advantage of the time to be themselves and share in the fun and excitement.

Certainly, camaraderie is one of the most important factors attracting party boat goers. But excitement and competition enter the game as well. Suspense builds as the day advances and each fish hooked holds the potential to become a contender for the "pool money" which, depending on several variables, can range from a few dollars to $2000 or more!

Little kids and adults alike sense this excitement and proceed to take curious "laps" around the ship to compare notes and take inventory of each other's catches. Then suddenly, word comes from the back of the boat that a really large fish has been taken -- the largest all week says the mate -- and the competition to beat that fish merely intensifies. For the fisherman, hope springs eternal!

Even on slow days, smiles and happy-go-lucky attitudes predominate, for how could one frown while relaxing on the water? Party boat fishing offers an antidote to cabin fever in the winter and year-round opportunity to enjoy nature in all her splendor as an occasional whale or porpoise surfaces alongside on a summer's ocean trip, or a flock of low flying geese saw overhead on a late fall bay trip. It also offers the chance to join a fellowship of smiles and conversation, or remain in the anonymity of a private world -- no questions asked. Finally, the opportunity to bask in the glory of winning the pool or being "high hook" caps the day. All things considered, the catching of a bucketful of good eating fish is an added bonus!

Chapter 6

⚓

Finding And Choosing Boats

Once sold on the prospect of taking a party boat trip, the first dilemma to be resolved is the choice of a target species. Virtually all other options, from the selection of a particular boat and tackle to making room in the freezer for your catch, stem from the answer to this question.

At certain times of the year, this decision will prove relatively simple. The months of December and January are a prime example. During this time of year those boats that sail in the northern and mid-Atlantic states usually choose to seek either ling and whiting or cod and blackfish while boats in more southern ports turn their attention toward grouper and red snapper. At other times of the year, however, several species of fish may be available. July visitors to Long Island's famed Montauk Point may, for instance, find it necessary to choose among bluefish, fluke, porgies and seabass, codfish or even tuna. Be aware, though, that one's options are always limited to those species for which any given party boat chooses to sail. If you're not sure which fish are in season, simply call ahead and ask. Most skippers will be more than happy to help you make a smart choice.

The best words of advice I can offer on this idea are to look, listen, and read. Local newspapers, fishing magazines, even T.V. or radio broadcasts, will help keep you abreast of the latest information on what's hot and what's not. Speak to local anglers and ask about their success.

If you don't know anyone who party boat fishes regularly, speak to the proprietor of your local tackle shop. He's sure to have at least some of the answers.

Perhaps the most reliable method for selecting a target species is to stop down at the dock and observe first hand the catches of several boats as they tie up at day's end. Ask a few of the patrons how they did and tell them you plan on going out soon. Oftentimes they'll offer all the free advice you'll care to listen to.

Sometimes, factors aside from availability will help determine your selection. Are you looking to fill the freezer? Then perhaps a trip for porgies will be best. If it's a hard fought battle and more excitement you desire, then a jigging trip for blues may be in order. How about a special trip to catch the bulldog of a lifetime over offshore blackfish haunts you could never reach in your own 14-foot skiff? Do you crave the taste of fluke fillets? No matter how well other fish are biting, this is always a tough one for me to pass up.

Keep in mind also the capabilities of those who will accompany you on the trip. If you intend to bring young children along on their first trip, fast action becomes a prime factor to consider. Party boat fishing for kids or beginners can become one of the greatest, or most boring and frustrating experiences of their lives. You can help steer it the right way by selecting the right species and conditions under which they will fish.

To many beginners, the open ocean may prove to be stronger than new found sea legs, and the strength and aggressiveness of large bluefish may leave them overwhelmed and more frustrated than excited. Generally, it's best to keep newcomers over bay or inshore waters even when fishing from a private boat. Remember, to the new fisherman action is what counts! Small, fast biting species such as flounder or porgies are always a hit with beginners. Understand that, especially when children are concerned, foregoing one or two "exotic" trips a season for more action may eventually pay off in the form of a lifelong fishing partner.

Merely deciding which species of fish to pursue will decrease the number of possible party boats on which you can sail. Still, making a final decision as to which vessel will bring you back to port with the biggest smile and fullest sack (although the two do not necessarily go hand in hand) can be quite difficult -- especially when you arrive at a port which has several ships sailing for your chosen quarry. The question that needs to be answered before making a decision is, "which party boat will best fulfill the needs of myself and my fishing partners?" To help answer this main concern, this section has been broken down into a series of simpler questions whose collective answers should help guide your final determination.

DO YOU HAVE YOUR OWN TACKLE?

Many private boaters will, especially for the inshore species. But if the answer to this question is no, then you will want to choose a boat which offers free or cheaply rented setups. Some boats have a fairly large selection of rods and reels available while others offer only a limited number. The average price for rented equipment varies from two to five dollars. On some open boats, a small security deposit may be required in order to protect the captain against loss or damage. As long as this deposit is reasonable, do not take exception to it. The skipper is merely attempting to protect his property.

Keep in mind also that some boats maintain their rental equipment in better condition than others. The smart fisherman will inspect each rental piece to be sure it is in proper working order. Should you find a faulty piece, merely return it to the mate or captain and request a re-

Most party boats these days are roomy and comfortable. Choosing one to suit your needs and wishes should not be difficult.

Scenes from party boating: A jumbo blue (top) that fell for a diamond jig with a surgical tube tail, and a bulldog black (left) that succumbed to a green crab. At right, anglers line the rail as they wait for action to start.

placement. In most instances your wishes will receive prompt attention.

IS THIS A FAMILY VENTURE?

If so, then a vessel with somewhat comfortable seating and working men's and women's facilities is to be strongly considered.

A second thought is to avoid fishing on a crowded boat. Aside from offering numerous opportunities to tangle and foul lines, a full boat may not have enough open spaces available for all family members to fish together. (Most patrons, however, will make room when asked courteously.)

If possible, attempt to plan family or group trips on weekdays as crowds will be considerably smaller and the mates will likely have more free time to spend helping novices.

HOW FAR AWAY FROM PORT ARE THE FISH?

If your quarry is more than a ten or fifteen mile boat ride from port, consider sailing from a ship located closer to the fishing grounds. Traveling by car to a closer port will decrease the length of the boat ride and increase the actual amount of time spent fishing. However, switch ports only when you reason that a significant amount of traveling time will be saved. There's no point in driving 40 miles to save 10 minutes when the fish are between ports.

HOW MUCH TIME DO YOU WISH TO SPEND FISHING?

At many ports, party boats can be found which offer half, three-quarters, and full day fishing. If you need to be home at a specified time, it may be advantageous to take a half or three-quarter day trip.

Should you be busy in the morning, many boats offer afternoon, evening, or night trips for various species such as weakfish or blues.

In the same vein of thought, boats leave dockside at varying intervals. Early risers will find 4:30 A.M. to 6:30 A.M. departures to suit their needs. For the late riser a 7:30 A.M. or 8:00 A.M. sailing time may seem more alluring. Some boats also offer afternoon, evening or late night trips. Be sure to make a mental note of the time the ship you finally decide to take is leaving port.

DOES DEPARTURE TIME COINCIDE WITH FAVORABLE TIDES?

Some days certain species of fish will decide to feed on a single tide or stage of tide. If reports indicate that your target species is feeding only

on the first half of incoming water, it may be beneficial to select a boat which will be spending most of its day on that particular tide. Sometimes, delaying your start by an hour can make all the difference in the world. No one enjoys sailing back to port just as the fish begin to actively feed.

ARE RESERVATIONS NECESSARY?
Some party boats require reservations at the height of the season or for special trips. While this is not usually the case, it may be a good idea to check ahead when sailing from an unfamiliar port.

DOES THE BOAT YOU ARE CONSIDERING ENJOY A GOOD REPUTATION?
Even if you usually fish from a private boat, you should have a feel for most of the local party boat choices. Is there a particular vessel that seems to always have a fun crowd on board when it sails past? Have you noticed one boat usually catching better than the others when

A List of Popular Party Boat Ports

Party boats can be found in every one of the northeastern and middle Atlantic states. The following is a brief state-by-state listing of some better known ports. Note that there are many locations harboring one or more boats which are not mentioned here. For a better idea of party boats in your local area, check the advertisements in local magazines and newspapers, or ask a local tackle dealer to recommend a productive port or boat.

MAINE:
Bar Harbor
Boothbay
Camp Ellis
Kennebunkport
Ogunquit/Perkin's Cove
Portland
York

NEW HAMPSHIRE:
Portsmouth
Rye
Seabrook

MASSACHUSETTS:
Gloucester
Green Harbor
Marshfield
Newburyport
Plymouth

RHODE ISLAND:
Narragansett/Point Judith
Snug Harbor

CONNECTICUT:
Bridgeport
Groton
Niantic/Waterford

NEW YORK:
Babylon
Bayshore
Captree Basin
Center Moriches
City Island
Freeport
Greenport
Howard Beach
Little Neck Bay
Mattituck

NEW YORK (cont.):
Montauk Point
New Rochelle
Orient Point
Point Lookout
Port Jefferson
Sag Harbor
Sheepshead Bay

NEW JERSEY:
Atlantic City
Atlantic Highlands
Belmar
Brielle
Cape May
Fortesque
Highlands
Hoboken
Perth Amboy
Point Pleasant
Sea Isle City
Wildwood

DELAWARE:
Bower's Beach
Indian River
Lewes
Mispillion Inlet
Ocean City

MARYLAND:
Chesapeake Beach
Crisfield
Point Lookout

VIRGINIA:
Deltaville
Lynnhaven
Reedville
Virginia Beach

you've been part of the mosquito fleet? If you are going to sail from an unfamiliar port, or are just not in touch with the fleet on a regular basis, ask around at dockside, check with friends or ask some of your local tackle dealers. Virtually any party boat worth its salt will have a small, loyal following of regulars plus a large contingent of repeat passengers. It's not difficult to get a pulse on the more reputable boats. Some boats enjoy a reputation for specializing in certain types of fish. Keep this in mind as you make your decisions. Remember, if you don't ask questions, you will not get the information necessary to make an educated choice.

Even after all the above is considered and debated, there is still that intuitive "feeling" which you get about each boat. Don't take this instinct lightly as in the long run, it will prove correct more often than not. With this feeling comes a sort of confidence in the skipper, crew, and boat itself, and with confidence often comes the desire, patience and drive needed to catch fish.

Chapter 7

⚓

Strategies, Tackle
And Other Insights

How many times have you heard the phrase "in the right place at the right time" used in describing a great play at a sporting event? More than a few, I'd venture. Well, the same phrase is often repeated on party boats, mostly by those who are not so lucky. But, as the die-hard sports fan will attest, this phrase rarely explains the entire scene. Smart strategy, good positioning, the right equipment and a knowledge of the rules can have a lot to do with creating one's "good fortune". With this thought in mind, let's take an in-depth look at some party boat fishing strategies, especially in relation to positioning. Then we'll briefly examine tackle requirements and some of the basic rules of party boat fishing.

Which spot on an open boat is best to fish from? That depends on the species and the method of fishing. While the age-old belief that the stern is the best spot certainly holds true at times, it does not necessarily follow that failure to procure a rail position at the back of the boat will doom one to a day of mediocrity. Based upon the method of fishing and local conditions such as wind or tides, the most advantageous position from which to drop a line does vary. It may even change during the course of your trip.

To be certain, the stern does offer its conveniences. Chief among these are protection from winds, more casting (underhand) room, a lessened chance of tangling, and proximity to the john. The stern's allure,

How Does the Skipper Find the Fish?

Ever wonder just how the skipper knows where the fish will be? It's not as complicated as you might think.

First, every skipper relies on his own experience and the fact that he is on the water day after day, constantly on top of the schools. Over several years of working an area, the skipper begins to learn the patterns that the fish take from year to year and season to season. Based on past results, he has a pretty fair idea of where the fish are heading when they begin to leave a particular area. Still, this knowledge isn't always enough so the skippers also rely to a large extent on electronic devices, especially when heading out into the open ocean.

One of the most important is a "Loran" unit. This device uses radio signals sent from various points along the coast to make exact readings of longitude and latitude. With it, a skipper can pinpoint the position of his boat anywhere to within 50 feet or so. This is a great help when working a small piece of bottom or a wreck that is out of sight of shore ranges. The skipper merely sails until the proper coordinates have been reached and he knows he is in the general area he wants to fish.

At this point, he turns on his depth finder or chart recorder to get an image of the ocean bottom directly under the boat. This will quickly identify any piece of bottom he wishes to work. If the boat is not over the exact spot he wishes to fish, the skipper may circle for a minute or two while watching the graph until the correct location is pinpointed.

Then there is the "fish scope". This tidbit allows scanning the water beneath the boat for schools of fish. These fish may also show up as "spikes" on the chart recorder, but on the fish scope they show up so well that a particular species or even individual specimens can be identified. This is a big advantage over guessing whether the fish on a chart recording are what you are searching for or simply bait. A major advantage of using the scope over the chart recorder when looking for the fish (from the skipper's standpoint) is the fact that the scope can be left on all day without running through several spools of chart paper.

Finally, all captains realize (or should realize) that they each have a vested interest in producing fish for their patrons. Thus, they talk to each other over the radios that each boat must have. If one captain finds the fish and the others are all striking out, there's a good chance he'll clue in the rest of the fleet.

however, probably originates in the fact that this is the position where the "gang" or "regulars" normally choose to meet. With many of the most experienced fishermen gathered in a single section of the ship, it often appears to the casual observer that this spot is providing the most action. After all, "everybody" seems to be connecting. Don't be fooled by this illusion. The number of fish taken directly reflects the skills and talents of these seasoned veterans. I have little doubt that if the regular gang chose to work the bow or midship, these sections would quickly be considered the choice real estate by the majority of the party boat crowd.

Basically, party boats employ five methods of fishing: anchoring over open bottom, anchoring over wrecks or structure, anchoring and chumming, drifting, and drifting with the aid of chum. Much of this is done in ways similar to those practiced by private craft. Because of the size of party boats and the number of anglers competing with one another for a limited supply of fish, however, an angler's station along the rail becomes much more important than your spot on a small boat. Party boaters positioned smartly to take advantage or the nuances of each different method of fishing are likely to catch the most fish. With this in mind, let's examine each method more closely from a party boat perspective and determine where best to make a stand. We'll start with the simplest: anchoring over open bottom.

Traditional flounder fishing is a good example of this procedure. Essentially, the skipper locates a piece of bottom known to harbor the target species, sets the anchor and signals you to commence fishing. With this method, each patron has a roughly equal chance of getting a bite as the fish are scattered in no particular pattern beneath the boat. Of course, those skilled in proper presentation and technique will, most times, eventually outfish the unskilled. All things considered, however, everyone has a fair shot at the fish. Fishing on the down-tide side of the boat will probably reduce the chance of crossing lines and thus, is the ideal place to set up shop.

Wreck or structure fishing differs from open bottom anchoring in that the boat is intentionally positioned directly above a specific object or break in the bottom contour. A ledge, sunken ship, or similar distortion is the usual target.

In this instance, midship is the safest position as the skipper tries to align his vessel with the underwater target. Ideally, the entire party boat settles directly above productive bottom, but changes in tide, current strength, or wind direction may be enough to swing the boat partially or even entirely off the structure. When this happens, you might as well be fishing in the kitchen sink for all the action you're likely to experience. Those still situated above the target will continue to catch while those shifted over open water will witness greatly reduced action. This holds especially true in the case of blackfish, seabass and cod as these creatures are very reluctant to leave the security afforded by structure. Fishing from midship increases one's chances of staying above selected bottom as the boat shifts through the course of the day.

Drifting requires more consideration and greater individual skill. As with anchoring, most positions along the rail have a fairly equal chance of hooking up. However, it should be noted that those at the head of the drift do get first crack at the passing fish. This slight advantage is somewhat negated by the fact that from this position, lines invariably drift under the boat resulting in a small amount of control and sensitivity loss. Those fishing the backside of the drift will find the fishing less exhausting as their lines should play straight out, resulting in greater feel, less frequent tangles and easier retrieves. To be fair, most skippers alternate from drift to drift giving all patrons the opportunity to fish both ways during the day's trip.

The downside of a drift offers first shot at the fish, but anglers must contend with lines drifting under the boat.

The addition of chum to any method of fishing can radically alter productivity around the rail. First of all, chumming increases everyone's chances. It does not, however, increase everyone's chances equally as many a bluefisherman will attest.

Chum is a term used to loosely describe any one of a number of concoctions deposited over the rail and into the current in the hope of attracting feeding fish to within reach of waiting anglers. It takes the form of, among other things, cracked skimmer clam or mussel, corn niblets or rice kernels, shrimp, fish chunks, or even a pastey soup made by mixing ground fish with water. In any form, chum always drifts downtide from the boat. From a fish's perspective, then, the food source is certainly located uptide, so most fish swim against the current as they follow the slick to its source, making those baits located downtide the first encountered. From an anchored, chumming boat the stern is the place to be provided the bow is facing upcurrent. On a drifting vessel, the obvious choice would be the downtide side.

In those instances where wind and tide collide, chum may move in seemingly odd directions, causing a shift in productivity throughout the ship. Be assured, however, that no matter how things appear chum always drifts with the current. One aspect of chumming that should never be overlooked is that chum does increase everybody's chances for success. Thus if one section seems to be getting the best of the action, remember that you're probably still doing better than you would have without its aid.

Just as important as proper positioning on a party boat is the selection of tackle that is up to the unique challanges presented by this kind of fishing. Although rental tackle is readily available on most vessels, the vast majority of regulars opt to bring their own. To be sure, there is nothing wrong with renting a rod and reel from an established boat. In most instances, the crew will set you up with tackle that is more than equal to the task. Sometimes, however, rental gear does leave a lot to be desired, so it's good practice to carefully inspect rod, reel and line before using any such setup. Be sure to check the guides for nicks and the drag for smoothness. Still, taking your own tackle on board is the best way to put your mind at ease, and it should also provide the confidence which familiarity breeds. As I mentioned in Chapter 3, I love to fish with four to eight pound test gear when conditions allow. It should be stressed, however, that light tackle and wimpy rods have no business on a boat where tangles and inexperienced fishermen abound. Due to the nature of party boat fishing, medium to heavy tackle is usually

Most party boats offer rental tackle and sell hooks and other accessories.

employed and baitcasting or conventional gear is usually preferred. Bay and shallow inshore fishing is the one instance where the use of spinning tackle is fully acceptable while party boat fishing, although conventional outfits still get the nod.

As described in Chapter 3, the biggest advantage to spinfishing is the ease of casting it affords. Keep in mind, however, that since overhead casting is not permissible on any party boat, this advantage is largely nullified. The greatest drawback to spinfishing is its lack of control. Light lines and limber rods simply cannot stem strong tides, so such lines are often pushed downtide by the current, crossing heavier, more stable lines in the process. The most common result of this situation is one big tangle with the lighter line interwoven among several heavier setups. If the tangle can't easily be resolved, guess who's line will be the first one cut? So if you are intent on using spinning gear, keep it a little on the heavy side. In fact, when party boating, it's probably a good idea to keep away from any setup spooled with less than 12 pound test.

There is, of course, more to tackle and equipment than rods, reels and lines but for other categories of tackle such as foul weather gear, coolers, etc., the needs of the party boater are almost identical to those who sail on private craft. Thus, for additional information on tackle and equipment needs, refer back to Chapter 3.

As you can see, strategy and suitable tackle, or lack thereof, can have a big influence on your score when party boat fishing. Also vital to success is a thorough understanding of the decorum expected from each individual who boards the boat.

All games have rules and party boat fishing is no exception. In order to ensure the safety and well being of all involved, as well as guarantee a pleasant and productive trip, certain guidelines have been established to which all should adhere. Those anglers newly acquainted to this manner of fishing will not find any of these codes stringent or difficult to follow. Neither should they find these regulations hard to remember as the majority are based on common sense and courtesy.

Personally, I think of these guidelines not as rules but rather as a code of etiquette which the refined fisherman will take pleasure in displaying. Integrating this code into your own personal fishing style will go a long way toward endearing you to rail mates. It will also make life easier for the captain and crew. In addition, your success in filling the bucket with finned creatures should improve substantially.

While fishing, especially under crowded conditions, try to keep in mind that both courtesy and smiles are contagious while at the same time, misery loves company!

Following is a general guide to party boat etiquette, most of which will pertain to any fishing situation. If followed, these rules should help make the day safe, productive and enjoyable for all.

TRY TO BE PLEASANT
Nobody goes fishing with the hope of having a bad time. One of the most unpleasant experiences an open boat fisherman can encounter is to find himself positioned alongside a real downer. If you know that your're in a bad mood, do us all a favor and keep it to yourself.

Should you find yourself fishing next to someone who is not in the best of spirits, make an attempt to spread some cheer. If the individual seems unresponsive or tells you in no uncertain terms that he does not want to be cheery, simply leave him alone or even move. By no means allow anyone in a foul mood to spread their gloom to you.

NO ONE EXPECTS YOU TO BE ST. PETER, BUT...
If you intend on keeping your sanity during the course of the day, remember that patience is a virtue. With anywhere from 10 to 200 lines dangling over the rail, strong currents and inexperienced fishermen, not to mention panicked fish, tangles are bound to occur from time to time. I can't for the life of me recall ever sailing on a party boat that went the full day without at least a few "good" tangles.

When your line comes up snarled in a mess of rigs appearing to be hopelessly tangled, just think of it as par for the course. Should the tangle prove too involved for you to resolve, call for the mate and he'll take charge. Most days the average angler should expect to be involved in at least three or four tangles. When fishing conditions become adverse, however -- as around full moon tides -- more frequent tangles are to be anticipated.

Can You Find The Pool Shark?

Finally, in the patience department, don't start complaining when the fish are not biting. The captain is trying as hard as he can to find the fish and he's probably just as disappointed as you are that the fish are not flying over the rail. Given time, most boats will locate fish. Be aware that sometimes even when the fish are found, they just don't want anything to eat.

WAIT FOR THE CAPTAIN'S SIGNAL BEFORE BEGINNING TO FISH

On all party boats, the skipper or his crew will inform the patrons when the time is right to commence fishing. Most ships use a single blast of the horn or whistle to signify the start of the day, but sometimes a verbal "go ahead" will be given.

In either case, it is imperative that you wait for this signal before lowering your rig. Failure to adhere to this warning will likely result in a real mess of a tangle that may well involve five or more people. The reason for this is that the boat must settle into its drift or anchored position before all lines will pay out directly in front of their respective owners. If you let your line down too early, it will drift off center, crossing other lines in the process. The tangles created in this way are some of the worst you will ever encounter.

From time to time as the fishing slows, the skipper may deem it necessary to move the boat to a new location. In this event, he will once again blow the whistle, signaling you to retrieve line. Reel up immediately so that the boat can get under way. If hooked up, don't panic -- simply hollar "Fish on!" The boat will wait until your battle is finished. When adequately repositioned in the new location, the skipper will send the signal to resume fishing. Three consecutive blasts of the horn indicate that the fishing day is over and the boat is ready to return to port.

WATCH YOUR LANGUAGE

This is especially so when you've been drinking alcoholic beverages. For many fishermen, party boating is a family affair. Please restrict your language in front of others and their families. Think how you would feel if you took your family out for a fun day only to have it spoiled by some nearby loudmouth whose entire vocabulary, it seems, consists of four letter words and other obscenities.

KNOW WHERE EMERGENCY EQUIPMENT IS LOCATED

Hopefully, the situation will never arise where application of emergency procedures and equipment are necessary. Party boating is one of the safest methods of fishing. Yet as we all know, accidents do happen on occasion. Knowing the exact location of fire extinguishers, life preservers, and first aid kits will help facilitate rescue or emergency operations under circumstances where a few seconds may mean the difference between life or death.

Take a few minutes when boarding any boat to investigate the whereabouts of all safety equipment. Should you never need to use it, you will at least feel secure in the knowledge that necessary items are close at hand.

KEEP THE AISLES CLEAR
It won't take long to notice that with everyone standing shoulder to shoulder at the rail, the pathway along the boat's perimeter is rather restricted. Make it a point to keep this aisle clear of coolers, tackle boxes, buckets and fish. On most party boats, equipment can be stored beneath the benches that line the outside of the cabin wall. If the ship lacks these benches, store all gear inside the cabin or at your side.

DO NOT FLIP LARGE FISH INTO THE BOAT
Wait for the net or gaff! More large fish are lost by anglers who, for one reason or another, decide to take matters into their own hands and attempt to swing or lift their prize over the rail. In addition to the probable loss of any fish lifted in this manner, the possibility of injuring nearby passengers is very real.

Naturally, if you are using suitable tackle a gaff or net should be unnecessary on small predators such as flounder, porgy, mackerel or blackfish. Larger species such as bluefish, weakfish or cod are a different story altogether.

When lifted aboard unaided, most fish weighing more than six or seven pounds will strain tackle past its breaking point. The most common result of this strain is that the hook bends, or simply pulls free, allowing your prize to fall back into the briny depths. From any fisherman's perspective this is disappointing. From a scientific standpoint it is downright dangerous! As Newton so aptly observed many years ago, "for every action, there is an equal and opposite reaction." The reaction in this instance is the resulting slingshot effect of the hook and sinker or lure (especially with diamond jigs) that sends them flying through the air, often back into the boat, possibly impaling themselves in the hide of some unsuspecting angler. So once again, wait for the net or gaff to assist you in bringing large fish over the rail.

If you should find yourself with a fish at the surface and a wait for the gaff (after all, the mate can only help one person at a time) by all means keep the fish completely submerged a foot or two. Lifting it out of the water even partially may give it just the leverage it needs to pull free from the hook. Just keep your line tight and remain calm. The mate will come to your aid as soon as possible.

A gaff is employed to help lift most large fish over the rail. Fluke, because of their body shape, and weakfish, because of their weak mouths, are usually netted.

NO OVERHEAD CASTING

The reasons for this rule, one of the most strictly enforced on any party boat, should be obvious. With so many people standing so close together, overhead casting is just too dangerous to allow. Besides, long casts are rarely necessary in the party boat game since the skipper usually positions the boat directly above any school of fish he locates. For the most part, the most productive waters to fish are those right below your feet! On those occasions when a cast may improve your results, underhanded "flips" will have to suffice. Keep this rule in mind, especially if you bring spinning gear aboard.

GET SEASICK OUTSIDE, NOT IN THE RESTROOM

I once knew a man who claimed vomit was some of the best bluefish chum available. When someone got sick at the rail, this fellow would

Pool Winning Tips

Theoretically, all patrons have an equal chance of winning the pool as they step aboard any party boat. Still, there is no denying that some sharpies seem to win more than their fair share of the pots. These anglers are experts in the field and usually take a few carefully calculated steps to increase their chance of landing the big one. Many anglers, novices included, hook fish that are big enough to cop the daily prize each day. The master fishermen, however, have usually taken care of all the small details that add up to landing a big fish. Thus when they do get their chance, they rarely miss. The novice on the other hand often finds a way to let the fish off the hook.

The following suggestions are simple ideas and checkpoints that most pool sharks make part of their daily routine. If you make sure to consider each tip, you too will increase your chance of getting that pool winner on deck.

1. Always enter the pool!
2. Sharpen all hooks before starting to fish.
3. Leave at least ¼" tag ends on all knots (except blood knots).
4. Use as little hardware as possible.
5. Never reel in against a fish that is taking out drag.
6. Play your fish until it's whipped. Green fish often break off at the boat.
7. Check your drag setting before starting to fish and recheck it after each hookup.
8. Check knots, line, and hooks for wear, fraying, or slippage every few retrieves and after each hookup. Retie and replace as necessary.
9. Let your rod do the work to sap the fish's strength.
10. Keep your baits looking natural and always allow for a fluttering tail when possible.
11. Bring along a bait that is different from the one supplied by the boat.
12. If more than one species is allowed in the pool, fish for the largest once you have caught enough of the smaller to fill your freezer.
13. Keep your fish iced down so they will retain as much weight as possible.
14. Never assume that your largest fish can't win the pool! For one thing, the big fish you saw taken may have been collected by someone not entered in the pool. For another, it may have been a species not allowable in the pool. Even if *five* fish bigger than yours were taken, it is possible that all five anglers were not entered in the pool.
15. *Never, never, never,* leave a possible pool winner in the sun. Doing so will find you muttering, "I coulda been a contenda" all the way back to port.

pull up his line and move right alongside. He won his share of pools too, although I doubt it could be attributed to the sickness of his fellow fishermen.

Seriously though, accurately hitting the "porcelain god" while staggering to and fro on a rocky boat is difficult at best. What's more, many people who vomit in the restroom are too drained to clean up afterward. Imagine how you would feel if you were next in line to use the facilities. Better to get sick over the rail where there will be no mess for anyone to clean.

DON'T BE A LITTERBUG

First of all, trash on deck gets slippery. Second, we all know our land and waters are not as clean as they once were and it's up to each and every individual to do his part to prevent our surroundings from getting worse. All party boats have or should have trash cans positioned in strategic locations. Use them! If there are no convenient receptacles, pack up your garbage and take it with you for later disposal. Never toss it over the side of the boat. Throwing trash overboard shows you are extremely lazy, don't give a damn, or both.

Some skippers specifically mention at the beginning of each trip exactly where the trash cans are located. This seems to heighten awareness among the patrons, ultimately resulting in less garbage being tossed overboard. Captains should go further in this direction, announcing at the start of each trip that no trash should be thrown overboard under any circumstances.

SHOW A CONCERN FOR CONSERVATION

There are few sights in fishing more depressing than unwanted fish left to rot at dockside. Although not a common occurrence it happens every summer, especially during the bluefish and mackerel runs.

Caught up during the heat of action, some overzealous fishermen keep all the fish they catch, only to discover at day's end that they have no use for 100 lbs. of bluefish or 225 lbs. of mackerel.

Keep only the fish you need. If you have room in your freezer for 100 lbs. of bluefish fillets, happy eating. If you don't have room for more than a few fish, give those extras to less fortunate fishermen or even release them. Don't be overly concerned with getting your money's worth in fillets. A few fish dinners along with the fun and excitement of your trip will more than cover the fee you've been charged.

A day in the life of a mate: (Top left) cleaning fish on the way back; (top right) securing the anchor; (right) weighing the pool fish; (bottom right) "pounding" up some flounder; (bottom left) gaffing a nice blue.

If by chance you find at day's end that you possess more fish than you have freezer storage space, consider giving leftovers to neighbors; or donate them to a local church or nursing home. I'm sure the folks there will enjoy the change of diet.

Bear in mind that, as with littering, should we allow children and newcomers to our sport to witness such abuses of our precious resources they may come to regard this behavior as acceptable or even worse, proper. Conservation is the key to the future of fishing. Let's make it a primary concern.

THE CAPTAIN'S QUARTERS ARE OFF LIMITS
The captain is responsible for running the ship and for the safety of all on board. He can't divert his attention to the questions of each patron and keep his mind on business. If you have a problem or need to see the captain, ask the mate to relay a message. Do not head into the captain's quarters on your own.

NO RUNNING, HORSEPLAY, OR SITTING ON THE RAILS
Because the deck is often crowded with patrons as well as sharp hooks and knives, running or heavy horsing around can endanger your health and the health of others. Stay in control and walk, don't run, wherever you need to go. Never sit on the rails of a party boat as the sea is unpredictable and one never knows when a wave that's a little larger than the rest is going to roll on by.

TIP THE MATES IF THEY DESERVE IT
It's very rare that a mate does not earn his or her keep. Even when the fish are uncooperative, the mates still have plenty of chores to attend. When planning your trip, assume that the mates will do a respectable job and plan to give them the customary 10% of the fare. If there is more than one mate, the tip is still 10% of the fare but it will be split by the crew. If you are lucky enough to win the pool, part of the booty (say 10%) should go to the mates if they deserve it. Give the tip to the first mate. Captains do not usually receive any gratuities. If service is unsatisfactory, bring it to the attention of the skipper and adjust your tip accordingly.

Part III:
The Quarry
And The
Technique

The following section details the specifics involved in catching some of the most popular species targeted by small boat anglers along the Northeast and mid-Atlantic coastline. While these are the mainstays, please note that anglers also fish for additional species in many areas (white perch, spot, redfish and drum come to mind) and from year to year local populations fluctuate, sometimes causing fishermen to redirect their efforts from one kind of fish to another.

There are actually two "sub-parts" within Part III, although they are not marked as such. These are inshore (Ch.'s 8-13) and ocean fishes (Ch.'s 14-17). The species in each grouping are listed in the order they arrive in our waters starting with the spring season. I should mention, though, that as with tackle, some areas tend to overlap. Blackfish, porgies and seabass, for instance, can be taken in bays, over inshore wrecks, and even mixed in with offshore codfish on occasion. Be aware of this overlap and feel encouraged to experiment and change tackle or methods when conditions warrant. Use this book as a guide, but keep in mind that nothing in the fishing world is ever written in stone. If your fishing expert friends or local party and charter skippers work the fish with different setups or methods than described here, go with it. They probably know what works on the fish in your neck of the woods a lot better than you or I. Showing a little initiative and trying your own ideas or the ideas of others will undoubtedly help to improve your score in the long run.

Chapter 8

⚓

Winter Flounder

Although some anglers may fish continuously throughout the year, in many areas the winter "blackback" flounder serves as both the first and final species of the season. Usually willing and numerous, flatties are targeted by private boaters, charter boaters and the party boat fleet during both early spring and late fall. In the more northern reaches of their domain, they may even offer fair sport through the summer months.

A rather uncomplicated sort which would rather lie in the mud than enjoy the cleanliness of a hard, sand bottom, this member of the flatfish family is neither difficult to catch (most days!) nor hard to land. It is part of a bountiful family of over 500 species, and proudly counts as close cousins the fluke and the mighty halibut. This latter predator can exceed 250 lbs. in weight with a body as wide as a picnic table and thick as a railroad tie!

Our pal the flounder is known as a popular bottom fish from southern New Jersey to as far north as Nova Scotia. While not truly a migratory species, they do move inshore and off each year as water temperature dictates. Their preferred temperature range is in the neighborhood of 50 to 55 degrees. Flounder spawn during the late winter and spring, at which time each female deposits roughly 500,000 eggs which cling together like miniscule clusters of grapes and sink to the bottom. Although the number of eggs seems to be more than enough, the flounder serves as a vital link in our local food chain and comparatively few attain maturity. The vast majority of flounder eggs are ravaged by small fish, crabs, and other egg eaters while young of the year fish serve as fodder for striped bass, weaks, snappers, blues and fluke. Even adult fish are not too large to entice a hefty bass or bluefish and, from time to time, you'll be reminded of this fact when a flattie you take has a huge scar or chunk of flesh missing from its side. As you can see, the flounder may spend a good deal of its time lounging in the mud of bays and harbors, but life for this flatfish is certainly no bed of roses.

As if things weren't difficult enough for the first year flattie, what with every bully on the block literally looking to take its head off, these fish must go through a "twisted childhood" before they assume the classic flatfish appearance. Flounder are born the same as any other ordinary fish, that is to say they swim vertically with one eye on each side of the head. Long about three months, however, the left eye begins to shift toward the right side of the head. While this optical migration is underway, the head bones gradually twist to one side and the body flattens out in a horizontal plane, taking on a dishlike appearance rather than gaining depth. By the time the left eye has finished its traveling, it comes to rest permanently beside the right eye. The body now begins to broaden, taking on the characteristic appearance of the flatfish. The top or dorsal side takes on a splotchy brown pigmentation providing a fair deal of camouflage protection while the bottom or ventral side remains stark white.

Although flounder may be taken throughout the year in some locations, most of the northeast and middle Atlantic states see two distinct peaks of activity. The first occurs in early spring, generally a week or two following St. Patrick's Day, and lasts through the end of May or early June. This strong run of fish is often called the "spring flounder run", but as with the "fall flounder run" which gets underway between late September and mid-October, the flounder we are speaking of are all one species. During the latter part of the spring run and early portion of the fall flounder season, sinker bouncers have the chance to take quite a few incidentals while fishing for flatties. Fluke, blackfish, blowfish, sea robins, tiderunner weakfish, and small blues often are taken by surprised spring anglers. In fact, as the water begins to warm and the flounder fishing slowly slacks off, many knowledgeable baymen fish cool, rising tides for departing flounder and warmer, falling water for newly arriving fluke. Thus, it's possible to bring home a mixed bag of

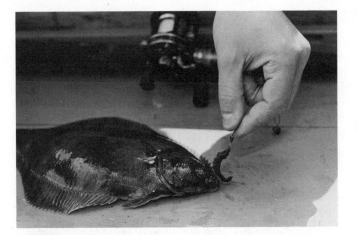

Flounder are very well camouflaged. Their underside is white while their dorsal side is a somewhat mottled brown (the brown will vary depending on the bottom). Notice the long, trailing bit of worm, wide gap style hook and light baitcasting outfit.

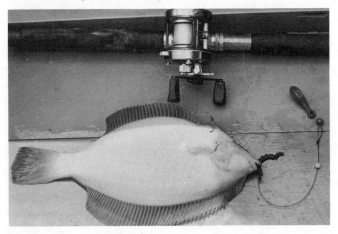

flatfish. During the early part of the fall run, blackfish, blues, porgies, sea bass, school weaks and an occasional triggerfish often wind up gracing the buckets of flounder pounders.

A common misconception about blackback flatties is that they are stationary fish. ("Blackback", by the way, is just a nickname for the winter flounder). According to this theory, they would rather wait for food to be brought to them (who wouldn't?) by the tide than expend energy in seeking it out themselves. While the theory may hold some weight early and late in the season when water temperature makes them sluggish, it rarely applies to flounder at the height of their run. In fact, having observed schools of flounder feeding in Moriches Bay and Montauk Harbor on Long Island, as well as having scuba dived among them, I would propose that nothing could be further from the truth. Flounder do actively seek out tidbits on the bottom. Each fish sort of crawls along supported by its length-long fins and moving its head from side to side as does a catfish on the prowl. They remind me of a small vacuum cleaner in the hands of a good housekeeper, actively seeking out each speck of lint hiding in the nooks and crannies of some vast, underwater living room carpet. The one difference is that these small vacuums need not go over the same tidbit several times! After watching these fish cover a fair amount of territory, it becomes apparent that they could easily wander several hundred yards in a single day should food not be plentiful enough for their liking.

During the spring and fall, flounder, with few exceptions, stick to inshore waters with a depth of thirty feet or less and mild to medium strength currents or tides. They are particularly fond of bays, harbors, estuaries, rivermouths, and even tidal creeks -- especially when these areas have a muddy bottom. Not overly discriminating, they will take up residence in any of the aforementioned locations as long as clams, mussels, sea worms, grass shrimp or other food sources are readily available.

Although winter flounder stocks seem to be a little depressed of late, these sporty bottom feeders are still quite catchable and their all around good nature make them an ideal species to kick off either the season or the fishing career of a beginner. Rarely will one need worry about getting skunked with these critters as catches of a dozen or more per angler are to be expected with some days easily producing two dozen or more. Although they put up a fair scrap for their size, it is rare indeed when a flattie manages to snap a line, throw the hook or cause any substantial tangles. This exceedingly good nature will help to keep the frustration levels of newcomers well below the boiling point.

Light to medium-light tackle is the most logical choice for flounder pounding and as long as the water is relatively shallow and sinker weights nominal, it matters little whether you select conventional or spinning gear. In water less than eight feet deep, I'll often try spinfishing, sometimes dropping down to a four or six pound test outfit when the fish get picky or when fun rather than food is on my mind. By the way, spinning gear for flatties is quite acceptable on open boats as the fish usually fight a straight up and down battle and do not often cross lines. If you are fishing from a party boat, however, keep the spinning gear to 12 lb. test or more just to be on the safe side. For general bay fishing, a five and a half to six and a half foot rod matched to either a spinning or conventional style reel loaded with 8 to 20 lb. test line will fill the bill on most outings. For ocean fishing or areas where tides run strong and water depth exceeds twenty feet, a slightly sturdier rod and stronger lines may be needed to control heavier sinkers -- but this is much more the exception than the rule in most locales.

Although a few boaters will try slow drifting when the fishing gets picky, most flounder fishing is done at anchor and, as far as rigging is concerned, the single most important factor to keep in mind is that flounder are strictly bottom feeders. This may not be news to the established bottom bouncer, but each season I am bewildered by the number of fishermen who drop high-low rigs or porgy setups over the gunwale and expect to fill their buckets with flatfish. I guess these fellas have just never had the opportunity to watch an experienced flounder pounder at work.

Most successful flattie fishermen I know like a two hook bottom rig with a pair of #8 or #10 long shanked Chestertowns tied tandem style just above a two to six ounce bank sinker as shown in the diagram. Since flounder can be plentiful, this setup frequently results in "double header" catches. If you prefer, a single hook bottom rig or slip sinker rig (see Chapters 9 and 12) can be substituted. Although I rarely use Chestertowns myself, they do make sense when the fish are biting with intensity because they hold baits well and are much easier to remove from a flattie's mouth than are most other hook styles. Having my choice, however, I usually opt for #8 wide gap style hooks as I feel that their ability to dig in and hold either a flounder or fluke is far superior to other varieties. Also, being somewhat lighter in weight than the Chestertowns, they tend to move about more freely when sitting on the bottom, occasionally waving and fluttering in the current and reacting to rod movements with a little extra pizazz (sproat hooks also work well). Some fishermen feel that the addition of a small yellow, red, green or pearl colored bead on the leader just above the hook helps to attract more fish. While this has never been the case for me, I mention the idea because it apparently does work at times.

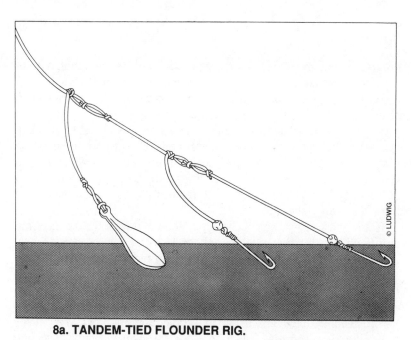

8a. TANDEM-TIED FLOUNDER RIG.

In the bait department, bloodworm, sandworm, mussels or slices of clam all have their followings. On party boats, skimmer clam or mussels are usually supplied but there are a few boats that may offer worms, too. It's a good idea to check ahead on this point as both sand and bloodworms are a little on the expensive side these days and taking out a boat which offers a choice of baits will cut down on your costs if you are a dedicated worm drowner.

It's been my experience that during the early part of the spring flounder run, worms are the most productive choice of bait. As the season warms up, however, bank mussels and skimmer clam begin to take precedence. During the fall season, the bivalves usually appear to have the edge. Some anglers use food coloring to dye their clams (usually skimmer) red or yellow the night before heading out and I've got to admit, these fellows rack up some impressive scores. Why these off color clams appeal to flatties is beyond me. All I know for sure is that they do out-catch regular clam on some days. A few anglers carry the flattie's fascination with color a step further and paint their sinkers yellow. Others even go so far as to strap small "light sticks" to the sinker via a rubber band. Both catch fish and both swear it's because of the added attractors. I don't know if either works for sure, but in any event

I prefer to keep my rigs as natural as possible. It does seem that, if nothing else, these added measures don't scare away many flatties.

When using worm baits, don't be afraid to string a two or three inch segment up the hook. Despite their apparently small mouths, even a postage stamp sized flattie can inhale such a piece and besides, the bigger fish definitely seem to prefer larger baits. Be sure not to bunch up that bait. Rather than hook your worm in and out several times, you should string it on the hook almost like putting a sock on a foot. Allow at least one half to one inch to trail free from the barb and make sure the worm hangs straight.

Clam baits, regardless of the type, should always be cut into thin strips and used by weaving the hook through each piece several times. As with the worm baits, leave a little trailing piece to act as an attractor. While skimmer is readily available at bait shops, I much prefer a thin, two-inch long strip of cherrystone or chowder clam. Usually, I'll pick up a dozen cherrys or half dozen chowders per fishing partner before heading out. These I keep in a cooler and open one at a time as the fishing day progresses. As long as they are kept cool and alive, any clams left over at day's end can be used to complement a plate full of fillets as baked or stuffed delights. If you run out of bait, there should already be enough fish in your cooler to send you home happy.

Mussels, a very popular bait in rocky waters, can be impaled in the same manner as are the clams, although these are much more difficult to keep on the hook. A trick used by sharpies when fishing this rock and structure loving bivalve is to shuck them and dry the meat out in the sun for half an hour or so. This makes the bait a little tough so it will stay on the hook better. The added toughness does not seem to deter any fish from striking.

It would be extremely difficult to overstress the importance of chumming to the successful flounder fisherman. All things being equal, the use of chum is what usually sets apart those who catch some flatties from those who quit early because they have several hours of filleting ahead. Popular flounder attracters include cracked steamer or skimmer clams, crushed mussels, ground clam or clam bellies, and corn niblets. I'm sure there are others, but these are tried and true. It should be noted, however, that proper deployment of the chum is vital to stacking flounder under your boat. No matter where one flounder fishes, it's best to put any kind of shellfish chum in a chumpot and lower it to the bottom. Ground clam is ideal for this application but will need to be

Knowing anglers get the chumpot over the side as soon as the anchor takes hold and the boat settles in. Double anchoring (from the bow only) will keep your boat and chum in line.

replenished every half-hour or so. Crushed mussels or clam do not as easily allow their flesh to pass through the mesh of a chumpot, and will, therefore, need less replenishing. A good combination is to put some crushed or ground shellfish inside the pot and also toss a few cracked mussels or clams uptide so they that they settle under your craft. Corn kernels make fabulous chum if you can get them to settle where they will do more good than harm. They are useless in deep or fast moving water as they are simply too light and quickly wash out of the chum pot or, if tossed overboard, roll or float down current and away from the target zone. In shallow or slow moving waters, though, such as those often found in coves or back bay areas, a handful of corn tossed up-current every five to ten minutes may be the best chum of all. Just to be sure that you are never caught completely chumless, you might want to stash a few cans of corn on board at the start of the season and keep them for an emergency.

Although chumming is routine among the small craft crowd, few party boats actually chum for flounder. On some vessels, the mate might pop around from time to time and stir up the bottom near your hooks with a plumbers helper lashed to a long pole, but that is usually the extent of chumming activities. It doesn't really matter, as the sheer number of baits in the water beneath these craft will usually act as attraction enough.

On certain days, flounder will attack a bait with vengeance, leaving little doubt in your mind that something is biting. Of course, these aggressive strikes must be considered in relation to body size and will not appear as much when compared to the strike of a bluefish or even a large porgy. Still, they are enough to let you know that the hook should be set if it hasn't already taken hold. At other times, flounder will hit so gently that only an experienced angler will know that one has sucked in the bait. At these times, it becomes important to employ what I call the "slow lift" approach. Upon feeling the slightest tap-tap-tap, which usually signals a pickup, lift your rod slowly until you can feel the weight of the fish just holding on the bottom. Now, lift another four or five inches and if there is a fish on the line it should try to quickly swallow the bait and dive back to the bottom allowing the hook to be solidly set. This technique takes a while to master but if you work at learning it your scores should easily double over the course of several excursions.

With the exception of Massachusetts' famed flounder haven, Quincy Bay, where many fish top the 2 lb. mark, and Block Island Sound and the east tip of Long Island, where occasional "snow shoes" may reach 4 or 5 lbs., the flatties you will encounter are likely to average between 3/4 and 1 1/2 lbs. Although flounder weighing over 6 lbs. have been taken from time to time, a 3 lb. fish is about the biggest most anglers see. But even average sized flounder are easy to fillet and the flesh of this flatfish is among the most highly prized of any east coast finster. Even though I have fished for much more exciting and exotic species, I still make several trips a year to stock my freezer with some of these delectable fillets. You probably will too -- once you have tempted and tasted this fish with a "twisted past".

Chapter 9

⚓

Blackfish
(Tautog)

Each spring and fall, this member of the Wrasse family journeys from deep water haunts slightly offshore into bays, sounds, inlets and shallow coastal waters. This movement is made according to water temperature, with the blacks trying to stay within range of approximately 52 to 60 degrees. They do not make an extensive north or south migration as do some other species such as mackerel or bluefish, but their travels are enough to cause inshore anglers to seek them twice a year rather than all year long.

Fall is generally considered the best time to make a blackfish excursion, as the fish then average larger than in the spring. Both seasons, however, can produce in quantity. Excellent table fare, the blackfish has firm light flesh which can be cooked in a variety of ways. This should come as no surprise when you consider that the blackfish dines on many of the more expensive items that you'd see on the menu of any seafood restaurant.

The immortal Matt Ahern has frequently written in his articles for *The Fisherman* magazine that the true measure of a master bottom fisherman is his ability to consistently catch blackfish. I agree completely, for these fish are indeed difficult to figure out. Once you begin to understand their feeding habits, though, I'm convinced that taking them becomes a much simpler task.

Bulldog blackfish, like this pool winner taken on a green crab by Arthur E. Wood (left), come huge on deep water wrecks.

Tautog, or simply "tog" to most New Englanders, are bottom dwelling creatures that feed primarily on shellfish, with blue mussels constituting the main dish on their menu. Because of this diet, they thrive in rocky or obstructed waters. Jetties, mussel beds, wrecks, underwater ledges, reefs, and bridge supports all harbor crabs and shellfish and thus are excellent bets to hold stable blackfish populations. Aside from being a private and rental boat favorite, blackfish are frequently targeted by the party and charter boat fleets.

The blackfish has two sets of teeth: a set of large buck teeth used for picking meals from their perch, and a molar-like set used to crack and grind the shells further back in its throat. Favoring locations with strong tides, the blackfish sets up shop in the densest structure available. Here it feasts, using its unique dental arrangement to crush and pulverize hard shelled items of delight. A real homebody, it will rarely stray more than a few feet from choice feeding grounds. Thus, fishing for this delicious bottom feeder is always done at anchor.

The combination of strong tides, dense structure, and this fish's unique dentures all contribute to the difficulty beginners experience when trying to hook one of these battlers. Complicating matters further is the fact that the fish's lips are exceedingly tough from picking up sharp or rough edged shellfish meal after meal, which does not make setting the hook any easier. Nevertheless, the blackfish is quite catchable if you apply yourself completely to the task at hand. And though it is certainly among the more cunning of bait stealers, it can be outwitted by even novice fishermen who learn from their early mistakes.

For bay or shallow water fishing, most boaters will find a six foot medium action rod coupled with a sturdy conventional reel to be a good choice. As blackfish tend to fight an up and down battle rather than make boat-length dashes, heavy spinning tackle can also be used, especially in shallow waters where the current is not too strong. A tough, high quality, abrasion resistant 12 to 30 lb. test line completes the outfit. Be sure to choose a line marketed as "abrasion resistant" if possible, as the terrain you will be working will often fray and strain even the best of lines.

Occasionally, some party boats may venture offshore on special blackfishing wreck trips. These are often made to deep water locations, where strong tides sometimes call for weights in excess of 16 ozs. In such a case, a sturdy cod rod should be substituted in order to allow you to control your rig and battle large bulldogs weighing as much as fifteen pounds.

The best fishermen often keep a finger on their line. This allows detection of even the slightest nibble.

As far as the terminal end of your rig is concerned, simplicity is the key. The more hardware you use, the greater your chances of snagging. To rig for blackfish, use a clinch knot to tie a 20 inch leader of 30 lb. test monofilament to a black barrel swivel. A three to four ounce bank sinker is then attached via an end loop. More or less weight can be used if local conditions mandate, but try to use the lightest sinker which will keep your line stationary on the bottom. A #2 to #6 Virginia style hook, connected to your line by a dropper loop roughly six inches above the sinker, completes the setup. The main advantage of using Virginia style hooks over other models used for blackfishing is that they are virtually indestructable. I use size #6 for most of my inshore fishing and have rarely seen one bend or break. But I will switch to a size #4 if I encounter fish of five pounds or more.

Many tog tuggers prefer to use a two hook rig. While I personally would rather keep my mind tuned on a single hook, when fishing in areas where the bottom does not eat up too many rigs (such as over a mussel bed) a tandem hook setup is perfectly acceptable. With either rig, it's a good idea to tie a simple overhand knot between the hooks and sinker. This will weaken the line below your hooks, allowing you to snap off the sinker should it become snagged. I've seen this little trick save more than a few 6 lb. plus tog over the years.

The preferred blackfish baits are fiddler, green or calico crabs though on party boats soft baits such as clam, squid or mussel are usually supplied. The cost of supplying crabs (especially green crabs) for party boat patrons is often prohibitive but most boats allow you to buy them on board and, of course, you can always bring along your own. Fiddler crabs are easy enough to use. Simply break off the large claw and in-

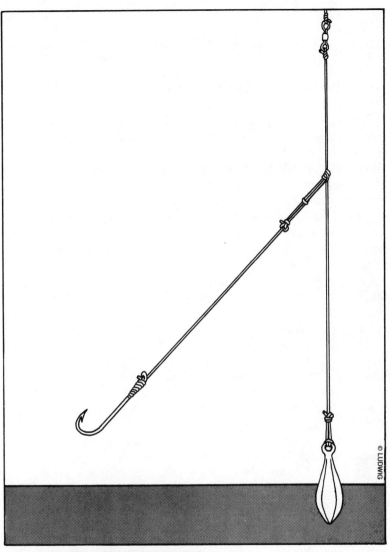

© LUDWIG

9a. STANDARD BOTTOM RIG.

sert your hook point through the exposed socket and out the rear. If the bait is small, string two or three of them on the hook. Green crabs or calicos require a little more work. Small ones should be cut in half and large ones quartered. To prepare for bait, remove the top shell and place the crab on its back. Next split it from front to rear. If it's large, divide each section in half again. Now, remove the legs and claws and insert the hook point through one of the claw sockets and out a leg socket. Be certain to expose the barb to ensure better hooking. If using clam or mussels, string them on the hook the same as you would for flounder but make the bait a little larger.

Although the baits noted above are the standards for blackfishing, hermit crabs undoubtedly reign supreme as the most dependable producer of tackle-busting sized fish. Unfortunately, they are almost un-obtainable from bait and tackle shops and the only way to be assured of having them is to gather them yourself. These crabs possess a soft abdomen that large tog especially relish. To rig them, begin by gently extracting the hermit from its borrowed shell. This is accomplished by pulling on the crab with steady pressure. If need be, the shell can be gently cracked and peeled apart until the entire creature is revealed. Next, insert the point of your hook just behind the head. Thread it under the back shell and down through the crab's abdomen. Pop the barb through the soft skin approximately halfway between the end of the back and the tail. As when using any crab bait, make sure that the hook point is fully exposed.

The myth of blackfish being caught by only the most experienced fishermen kept me from trying for them for years when I was younger. True, the most seasoned anglers will easily double the catch of some novices. But if the masters are pulling in twenty fish a day, there is so reason a first timer can't catch ten or twelve once getting the hang of it. Remember, the only way to become an expert is to get out and take your best shot a few times. Once hooked on blackfishing, many anglers become fanatics.

The key to hooking blackfish is patience. These fish signal their interest in your offering through a series of sharp pecks as they grasp your bait with their front teeth. These pecks are soon followed by a sharp downward tug as the bait is passed down their throat to the crusher teeth. Wait for the tug before trying to set the hook. The temptation to set the hook on the first peck is great, but with a little determination it can be overcome. Remember to set that hook hard, as tog have tire-tough mouths. Once the hook has been set, keep the rod held high to prevent the fish from diving back among the rocks or other structure.

During the spring run, most blackfish taken average a pound or two with a few old soakers mixed in to keep the action interesting. When the fall season arrives, the average size of the fish taken increases some-

Hermit crabs (left) and green crabs (right) are the undisputed top producers of big blackfish. At bottom is a classic blackfish scenario—anchored along a rocky jetty.

what and the incidence of six pound plus fish rises sharply. While the fishing during both seasons is basically the same, it should be noted that blackfish seem to prefer mussel beds and scattered structure during the springtime, wrecks and dense structure during the fall.

The blackfish is a dogged fighter which will resist every inch of the way to the surface. In fact, fish of eight or more pounds are termed bulldogs in recognition of their fighting ability. While they may not be among the easiest fish to hook, one thing is for certain: Ugly and tough as this brawler may be, few fish taste sweeter or look better on the dinner plate.

Chapter 10

⚓

Striped Bass
(Rockfish)

Big, powerful, pretty, delicious, a predator willing to take lures or bait from the surface to the bottom under moon or sun: the striped bass is a wonderful gamefish embodying all that is valued by recreational anglers. No fish common to our coastline enjoys more loyalty than does the regal striper -- she is truly the queen of inshore waters.

Easily recognized by the seven to eight rich, black, horizontal lines which run the length of its silvery flanks the striper, or rockfish as it is called in southern waters, is both anadromous and migratory. Originally, its distribution was confined to east coast waters between northern Florida and Maine. Today, though, the striper is also pursued in the Gulf of Mexico, along the west coast off Oregon and California, and in many of the larger freshwater impoundments of the south and west. In most of the salt water locations, striped bass range in size from schoolies of 2 to 12 lbs. to cows that may exceed 60 lbs. in weight. Bass of 15 to 30 lbs. are fairly numerous in some waters and most areas see at least a few fish in the 40 to 50 lb. class taken each season. Females tend to grow larger than males, with most fish over 25 pounds being ladies. While freshwater stripers may grow nearly as large in some instances, they tend to average a good deal smaller than their briny based brethren.

Studies indicate that the main stock of east coast bass are spawned in the freshwaters of the Chesapeake estuary. Most of the smaller and mid-sized bass also return here for the winter. Some larger bass, however, may choose to spend the colder months in deeper ocean waters off the Carolina coasts. By mid-April, school sized bass spread forth from their estuarine wintering grounds to probe the coast between the Carolinas and New York in search of worms, shellfish, crabs, and baitfish. The larger bass usually arrive inshore between late May and early June as water temperatures hover between 60 to 65 degrees. A true littoral species, the striper rarely strays more than a dozen or so miles offshore and spends most of its time within a mile or two of the beach in water depths of 6 to 80 feet.

Apparently, there are at least two separate strains of stripers mixing in our waters. The predominant Chesapeake strain noted above is a roamer, traveling as much as 350 miles north or south of its wintering grounds before heading back during the fall. A second "ravine" strain of bass, typical of those spawned in the Hudson, Navesink, Delaware and several Carolina rivers is more of a homebody, moving out of bays and along the coast perhaps 60 to 100 miles at most. The two strains of bass are indistinguishable to most anglers but biologists can tell them apart through scale and tissue samples. Some claim the traveling Chesapeake strain has a more streamlined appearance.

Traditionally, the waters of Chesapeake Bay have contributed up to 80% of all Atlantic stripers but, alas, this great fish factory has fallen on hard times. As has been widely documented and publicized, the Chesapeake hasn't produced a truly dominant year class of bass since the 1970's. Yet, isolated populations of non-Chesapeake bass, most notably Hudson spawned fish, have been doing well, providing good to very good fishing in localized areas. For example, the 1980's have witnessed the most productive bass spawns ever recorded in the Hudson estuary and anglers in northern New Jersey, Long Island and south-western Connecticut have enjoyed very good action with school sized fish. Unfortunately, even doubling the productivity of these lesser con-tributors isn't nearly enough to make up for the lack of Chesapeake fish when one looks at the picture with a coastwide, long term view.

Due to its diminished numbers, the striper is under tight regulation up and down the coast. The driving force behind the restrictions is a need to protect the strong (but not dominant) year class of 1982, and subsequent classes of Chesapeake bass, in the hope that they can

Few fish are more impressive than a cow bass. Charter skipper John Alberta took this 70 lb. trophy on a live eel drifted off Montauk Point, NY.

produce another dominant year class. As such, every state between Massachusetts and North Carolina has at least some minimum size and/or possession limit on these popular gamefish. Some, in fact, have instituted a total moratorium on the keeping of bass, so before heading out give local regulations a check. Ironically, while the striper is having a difficult time within its natural boundaries, it is thriving in many freshwater locations where it has been transplanted. To date, bass close to 60 lbs. have been taken from "sweet water" impoundments and it's only a matter of time until a fish challenging the salt water world record of 78 pounds 8 ounces is boated.

One aspect of the striper's personality that so endears it to anglers nationwide is its willingness to strike at a wide variety of offerings. "Linesiders" from schoolies to cows will fall for jigs, bucktails, trolled seaworms, tubes or spoons, cast plugs and poppers, or chunk or live bait such as eels, bunker, mullet, spot or herring, most of which can be presented either at anchor or on the drift. In some backwater situations, bass will even succumb to small poppers or streamer flies twitched through their territory by stealthy fly fishermen. Whole volumes have been written on bass fishing alone and for lack of space I'll not attempt to cover each possibility in depth here. I would, though, like to offer a few ideas on techniques that produce bass during the different seasons.

In Long Island Sound where I do a good deal of my early season striper fishing, the first fish of the year traditionally fall to bank fishermen offering whole sand worms that are anchored by standard bottom or fish-finder rigs. I'm sure the same scenario is repeated at various locations up and down the coast. Within two or three weeks of these first reported catches, slow trolling action begins to kick in. This usually occurs in shallow (four to eight foot) depths where a whole worm carefully threaded up the shaft of a #5/0 or 6/0 O'Shaugnessy or beak baitholder style hook (and proceeded by a small willow-leaf spinner blade) is often the favorite ticket -- especially in areas known to harbor steady populations of school bass. This trolling is done exclusively at night, when the stripers are most apt to work the shallows close to shore with channel edges, grassy flats near sharp embankments, back coves and boulder strewn beaches all proving to be choice real estate. As the waters begin to warm and May moves into June, the bass also begin to respond to small 5 to 5 1/2 inch Rebel, Rapala, Bomber or Helcat type minnow immitations. If they are "slapping" on top, it may even be possible to take a few on tiny poppers or fly fishing gear. In all three cases, calm, windless nights produce best, allowing for clear water conditions that make it easy for the fish to see, hear or smell your baits or lures and, thus, zero right in on them.

If you would like to take a bass on spinning tackle, this is the time to do it. With the fish in shallow water where tides are usually minimal, 8 to 20 lb. test setups are ideal for trolling worms or, especially, casting plugs. Be aware, however, that there is always the possibility of tangling with a bass of 20 lbs. or more, even early in the season. If you fish in an area where big bass are known to roam, or where boulders are more numerous than the fish, you might want to keep your spinning tackle a little on the heavy side. As a rule (oft broken), casters drift with the tide while trollers move ever so slowly against it.

With the approach of the June full moon, striper populations should be well established both in the bays and along the oceanfront. It is now that the first big bass of the new season begin to make an appearence. While these fish can be taken on bunker and mackerel chunks, or by working live bait or plugs tight to the beaches, the most outstanding catches at this time of year are more often decked by early morning wire liners trolling umbrella rigs. Especially productive are deep channels in and around inlets or river mouths.

The standard tackle for this action is a 40 lb. test conventional setup with 40 lb. test stainless wire line and a twenty foot length of 60 lb. test mono leader preceding the umbrella. One trick that seems to really increase the productivity of umbrella rigs is to add a 12 to 14 inch length of mono leader between the surgical tube lures and stems of the rig. Some store-bought umbrella rigs will come with 8 to 12 inch mono leaders above each tube but others come with the tubes attached directly to the stems. Increasing the leader length puts the tubes back a bit from the stems and I think it really does help to make the bass a little less suspicious. I usually make all but one of my leaders the same length. The oddball is one of the tubes that will be on the bottom of the rig as it is trolled. I'll pick one tube and add to it a leader twice as long as the others. This sets that tube back a little further than the rest, making it look like a struggling minnow trying to keep up with the school. On slow days, the trailing tube often takes all my fish, while on good days it usually takes the largest bass. When trolling for bass you'll usually do better if you randomly increase or decrease your speed a little bit from time to time. This will cause your lures to rise and fall in relation to the bottom. A faster speed brings the lures up toward the surface while decreasing trolling speed allows them to drop closer to the bottom. Working a varied pattern also seems to help.

In general, it's a good idea to keep all the tubes on an umbrella rig the same color and size (i.e., all three-inch green tubes or all five-inch

Small boats, quiet nights and school stripers are a frequent mix in some areas. Casting light plugs is one of the author's favorite pursuits.

red tubes) as different size tubes require different trolling speeds to work just right. Although umbrella rigs may have anywhere from three to a dozen tubes, those carrying four to eight lures seem to produce best and tangle least. In most situations, 150 feet of wire will get your rig into the strike zone but when the fish are feeding deeper than 20 feet, you might need to let out 200 to 300 feet. Green, red and black tubes all have their days but overall white has been my best bass producer.

The summer months with their high temperatures can be a tough time to take bass but there are some anglers who still manage to do it consistently. One way to score is with a technique known as clam chumming, a time-honored art that seems to have been all but forgotten in recent years. Only twenty years ago, when stripers were more plentiful, it was common to see two or three boats anchored just uptide of many bridges spanning inlet or channel waters, each doling handfuls of clam bellies out into the current. Back then, catches of a dozen bass a tide were the norm and some days saw as many as 20 to 30 fish come aboard. Those were the glory days of bassing when 20 and 30 pounders were chummed with surprising regularity and cows of 50 lbs. even graced a few decks during July and August. Those days are gone now, and a good day of clam chumming under present conditions is a half dozen to a dozen fish, mostly schoolies and teens. Still, that's better than most other methods will produce during the sweaty "dog days". I've personally caught bass using this method when afternoon temperatures exceeded 100 degrees! Why is this technique so productive in the summer? I'm not quite sure, but I suspect some of its appeal to the bass is that the food comes to them on the tide and they have to do little or no chasing after their meal.

Essential to chumming up summertime bass is first finding a resident population of fish. You can ask around, but it's hard to pry hotspots from the jaws of secretive striper fanatics. A better way is to take a trip to the library and scan through some back issues of local fishing magazines or newspaper columns. Check over fishing reports for the months of June, July and August from the early to mid 1970's. Back then there were so many bass around that it wasn't vital to keep every hotspot a secret and word often got around as to where the fish were feeding. Chances are any structure listed in those old reports as holding bass will still draw a few today. You'll be surprised at the places that turn up. Often it will be a bridge or hole that every boating angler must pass by on the way to favored grounds for other species.

Probably the most difficult aspect of clam chumming today is finding a reliable source of bellies. Due to lack of demand, most tackle shops no longer stock this bait. Many shops can, however, get it if given a few days notice. Clam bellies are sold in five gallon cans and run $10 to $12 per barrel. One barrel is usually good for three or four anglers working a single tide.

Assuming you can procure a can of bellies and have a beat on some fish, the next step is to anchor up and start a chum slick. Once in position, begin chumming by grabbing an even handful of clam bellies, holding them over the water and squeezing out the juice. Then let the clams slide out of your hand one at a time so that they drift out in a small trail about six feet long. Always drop the clams from the same corner of the boat so that they drift back into the same place in the slick. Let a handful go every four or five minutes. To ensure that the slick is consistently in the same location, its a good idea to double anchor.

Rigging for clam chummers is refreshingly simple. A three or four foot length of 15 to 20 pound test mono leader is snelled on one end to a 2/0 to 4/0 bronze or gold beak (baitholder) style hook. The opposite end is adorned with a #3 or #5 barrel swivel. The end with the swivel is then tied to the main line via a clinch knot. Don't try to use a rig without a swivel, as retrieving a baited clam rig against the tide will cause your line to spin. This can result in twisted line that will constantly want to knot up on your reel. With the swivel, only the leader will spin and your line should remain in good condition. Because of the possibility of big fish and strong tides in the areas you'll most likely work, conventional setups in the 20 lb. class are favored for this kind of fishing.

Once the rigging is completed, weave several clam bellies on the hook and an inch or two up the line. The bottom clam is hung loosely from the hook so that two to four inches of stringy ends hang free and will undulate in the current. Be sure that the hook barb protrudes from the toughest section of the last clam. Don't be afraid to use three or four bellies at once. You want the clam to have some weight so that it will quickly sink in the tide.

At this point you are all set to go. No casting is necessary as the line is simply stripped off the spool at a rate faster than the current to start the baited hook on its drift. Once 20 to 30 feet of line is peeled off the reel, the current should begin to carry your bait and you can then free spool out the rest of the line. Be sure to keep a thumb to the spool to prevent over-runs.

Line is played out into the current until the bait stops (indicating a hit or the bottom) or until it has drifted back more than 150 feet. If you feel a pickup, allow the slack to tighten out of the line and sock the fish quickly to prevent deep hooking your quarry. If no hit occurs, reel in and begin the process again. If the current is very strong, you might need to add one or two 1/4 ounce rubber core sinkers to the top third of the leader to get your line down into the strike zone. It is often necessary to experiment with various amounts of weight and line lengths before the right combination is discovered. Once you connect, the fishing should be fairly consistent. Occasional adjustments may be necessary as the tide grows stronger or slackens. In most places, the best clamming scores come on the first or last quarter of outgoing water. Interestingly, the bass tend to station themselves slightly *uptide* of most structures when taking up positions in a chum slick. Your boat, then, should be anchored 100 to 150 feet uptide or up current of the structure you intend to fish.

As you can see, bass can be taken throughout the spring and summer months, but it is during the fall months of September, October and early November when bass of all sizes migrate simultaneously along the Atlantic surfline on their way back toward their wintering grounds. It's at this time that the blood of bass anglers really begins to boil. Many anglers, in fact, take more bass during two or three weeks of fast fall action than they do throughout the rest of the year combined. Certainly, it is during this period when the majority of cows are boated.

As late summer fades to fall and the first northeast winds begin to add some snap to the air, migratory baitfish begin to bunch tightly and slide in tiny pods ever southward. As they move down the coast, dropping tides at each new inlet and rivermouth add their contribution to the parade, swelling the ranks into solid schools and, eventually, stretching them into one almost continuous ribbon of striper fodder. With what appears to be at times a giant sized chum slick spreading down from Massachusetts toward North Carolina, the bass need no prodding from fishermen to turn on.

It is now that trollers go to work, and often reap their just rewards. Some work eel-sized tubes or white bucktails tipped with a healhy strip of porkrind. Others pull Danny plugs through the roughest of rips, while still others drag giant bunker spoons for miles and miles along straight, unbroken sandy beaches. It is also now that traditionalists drift live eels, bunker, mullet or herring on falling tides through inlets and channels in the hopes of taking the fish of a lifetime -- a cow bass of over 50 lbs.! During the fall, as many fish are taken during daylight as at night, especially in October and November.

Live eels, fished with or without a small drail, account for many of the biggest linesiders. Here, Lorry Mangan prepares to drop a "snake" over the side with high hopes. Hooking the bait through the jaws helps keep it alive and reduces tangles.

Few feelings in fishing can match the anticipation felt by a live bait angler whose offering has just been picked up. As he feeds line into the current a thousand thoughts tumble through his head. Most of these center on not making a mistake, but always in there somewhere is the dream that maybe this is the big one. As the boat and fish drift in opposite directions for forty or fifty feet and the reel is finally engaged, the angler is a study in total concentration. Then he feels it and the rod takes on a solid set. It's a good fish, but no world record. But the reverence accorded this species is such that even a big schoolie is given the respect usually shown only to the largest specimens of lesser gamefish.

The live bait fisherman can employ any of several rigs to take stripers. "Eelers" will find that a #7/0 short shanked tuna, siwash, or O'-Shaugnessy style hook attached to the end of a 30 to 60 lb. test mono leader (equal to the length of the rod) is all that is needed in shallow waters. For deeper action, a two to six ounce drail may be attached to the main line ahead of the leader. Remember to place a #5 black barrel swivel at the head of the leader. On this rig, a "shoestring" eel measuring 8 to 16 inches long is impaled by hooking it through the eyes or both lips. Why the long leader? Two reasons: 1) It allows the angler to raise his rod high while a big bass is being gaffed, eliminating the need to haul the fish close to the boat by hand in order to stick it, and; 2) On those nights when there is "fire" in the water, the extra length puts some distance between your bait and the "sparks" touched off by the drail as it activates the tiny bioluminescent creatures which often seem to make feeding stripers uneasy.

For those dunking bunker or similar large baitfish, a 3/0 to 4/0 XXX stout treble can be secured to the end of a 48-inch length of 40 to 50 lb. test mono leader and the hook placed just ahead of the dorsal fin. Without a drail, this rig is an excellent choice for working back bay waters, shallow beach sections just beyond the breakers, or eddy areas of inlets and rivermouths. With a drail added as described above, the same rig will take fish holding in deep water sections of fast moving inlets or ocean rips. With three points the chances of hooking up are significantly increased. Better still, anglers need "drop back" only a few feet on pickups, reducing the number of gut hooked bass. Finally, some anglers like to work a slip sinker rig with the same short-shanked tuna or #7/0 O'Shaugnessy described above. Such a rig can be used to work either eels or baitfish in areas of moderate current or water depths of 20 feet or less. For the last two baitfish rigs noted, a stinger hook may be added. As you've probably figured out, conventional gear in the 20 to 40 lb. class range with a fairly stout six to six and a half foot rod is the usual choice for this kind of fishing.

Note that no wire leaders are used with the rigs described above. Wire leaders almost always seem to reduce striper strikes. When big bluefish are abundant, this will obviously prove to be a problem. In such situations, you'll have to make a decision: either fish though the blues and lose several rigs, or add a six inch length of wire and run the risk of turning the bass off.

Not everyone has the patience to dunk bait. If more work is what you desire, diamond jigging is a productive and exciting way of taking fall run striped bass. Similar to weakfish, stripers will often cruise beneath marauding schools of choppers, feasting on mangled baitfish that flutter to the bottom. At such times, a four to eight ounce diamond jig worked slowly beneath the blues will produce solid catches. While the blues will hit the jig from time to time, your chances of catching bass will increase greatly if you work the jig slowly within five feet of the bottom and select a lure sparsely tipped with white bucktail rather than one trailed by a surgical tube.

With striper stocks still at very low levels coastwide, conservation must be practiced. The various state regulations currently in effect should ensure that anglers return most of their catch to the sea. What we must concern ourselves with, then, is making sure that those fish released are put back in satisfactory condition. To this end, cut the line on any bass for which your hook cannot be easily removed and avoid using stainless steel hooks. If you choose to fish with bait, its a fact of life that some fish will get the hook in their gut. In this case, cut the line. A new hook costs only a quarter or so; a striper once removed or killed is irreplaceable.

Before releasing, make sure any fish you intend to return has recovered from its ordeal. Small fish can often be released without being brought into the boat. Larger fish can be *carefully* gaffed in the lower jaw and gently slid aboard. Handle the fish as little as possible while it's out of the water. A fish showing signs of exhaustion (i.e., laying on its side) can often be revived if you face it into the current and support the fish by the belly and tail for a minute or two before releasing it. When the queen is ready to return to her watery kingdom, they'll be no holding her back.

Chapter 11

⚓

Weakfish
& Sea Trout

Although many anglers refer to either of these species simply as sea trout, the weakfish and spotted sea trout are not quite one and the same. They are, however, first cousins and the methods and tackle used to tame one will often work on the other. To keep the reading smooth, we'll concentrate on the weakfish here, noting appropriate sea trout information where pertinent.

Weakfish are the ghosts of east coast fishing. Caught by the thousands during the early 1970's, these speckled beauties are currently experiencing a drastic population decrease, especially in their more northerly haunts. Apparently caused by a combination of factors including indiscriminate commercial netting and a traditional cyclical population pattern, this decrease seems to have caused weakfish to become much more selective in their feeding habits as well as harder to pin down during the course of their migrations. This is probably due to the fact that a smaller population of fish equates to less competition for food and thus the fish can overlook any bait that appears unnatural.

Back in the early 1970's when weakfish populations were at their peak, it seemed all one had to do to hook up was drag a plastic tailed lure behind a drifting boat. Nowadays, inexperienced fishermen rarely score well with large weaks and a catch of three or more fish per person on a single trip is considered a very good day north of Delaware Bay. Fortunately, it is still possible to have a fair time with summer run schoolies or "spike weakfish" in some areas, but most often now the majority of the catch on a weakfish trip are incidental species such as sea robins, fluke, sea bass, kingfish or cocktail blues. Hopefully, strict management of the remaining stocks and a natural upturn in the cycle will allow the fast paced spring fishing to return once more.

The reason I refer to weakfish as "ghosts" is not because of their decreased numbers, but rather the manner in which they quietly come and go as they seek their meals. During waking hours, action could best be described as a steady pick. There are few daylight blitzes and weakfish do not relish chasing bait on top when the sun still shines (as bluefish are wont to do from time to time). In fact, most fishing for this species is done during evening or nighttime hours, and that includes party boat fishing.

Although its body shape, eyes and mouth structure are remarkably similar, the spotted sea trout is easily distinguished from its close cousin by its larger, well spaced spots. While the weakfish appears to have freckles the sea trout sports a handsome polka-dot pattern. Both fish are trout-like in appearance and pleasing to behold. Size can also be a distinguishing factor between the two; while the weakfish can attain weights exceeding 18 lbs. and averages six to ten pounds, spotted sea trout rarely exceed ten pounds and average two to four pounds. Still, in waters where the two species mix, such as southern New Jersey or the DelMarVa region, the two are sometimes confused, especially in catches of school sized fish.

Since male weakfish and sea trout have the unique ability to emit a croaking or drumming sound by vibrating their abdominal muscles against their air bladders, these fish are sometimes called croakers. Such sounds are usually made in anger or fear, or to attract mates during breeding season.

While some sail for weakfish during daylight hours, evening and nighttime departures are usually more productive. It is at night that these fish can be observed silently cruising that eerie zone where a boat's bright lights melt into the night's deep darkness. Rarely are the fish seen in their entirety. Rather, their silhouettes are barely discernible to a trained eye as they slip by at a casual cruising speed, occasionally turning their head or even rolling their body slightly to inhale a chunk of chum, small baitfish, or even a hook. The fishing can be especially good for those who quietly work the shadow line of a bridge or similar lighted structure. At such locations, shrimp and baitfish gather to feed near the surface in the artificial light cast upon the water from above. The weaks,

Inlet livelining accounts for some mighty big weaks, especially in early fall. Small snappers and bunker are favorite baits.

in turn, prowl just below the bait or at the edge of the darkness, waiting to ambush any prey that happens to cast a careless shadow too far from the protection of the structure. Night fishing, by the way, can be intriguing regardless of whether or not the weakfish decide to cooperate as it affords the opportunity to observe squid, skates, bats and other nocturnal creatures which are rarely seen during waking hours.

Weakfishing north of Delaware Bay is usually a spring affair, for it is at this time of year that the greatest number and largest fish flood bays and estuaries in preparation for the spawn. They will eat little, if at all, until this biological urge has been satisfied. Once spawning has been completed, however, these fish go on a feeding binge as they try to replenish their depleted energy levels and fat reserves. This usually occurs when the water temperatures are between 60 and 70 degrees. Good fishing may last up to a month but in recent years has tended to hold up only two weeks or so. Since weakfish prefer water depths of less than 40 feet during their inshore stay, the hottest action often takes place within a short ride of port. Weakfishing in the Chesapeake Bay region gets under way in late April and picks up later as you head north. Long Island's famed Peconic and Great South Bay fisheries hit their peak around the end of May. As the waters begin to warm, the larger weakfish break into small pods and work their way back out to the open ocean. The tight schools of spring slowly dwindle until mostly small, school sized fish remain in the bays. With the weaks now scattered, it's hard to produce enough to justify sailing and so most anglers switch over to other species. In Delaware and Chesapeake Bays or waters further south, however, fishing for summer schoolies and sea trout is just getting underway in early summer.

DICK MERMON

Sea trout can be distinguished by their trout-like shape and polka-dot pattern.

Spotted sea trout spawn in inshore waters from April through November with peak activity usually occurring from late May through early July. The further south you head, the earlier the spawn gets underway. Although they are occasionally caught as far north as Long Island, NY, the largest concentration of sea trout along the east coast is found between Florida and North Carolina. It should be noted that spotted sea trout are much more plentiful within this range than weakfish are in their home waters these days. Sea trout are also available for a longer part of the season, and are not quite so shy about feeding when the sun shines. These traits cause them to be much in demand well after the weakfish have, for the most part, departed.

Like the weakfish, large sea trout prefer to hold over channel edges or close to structures where strong currents will disorient baitfish. Smaller sea trout, however, seem to like better the quiet waters of back bay and drainage areas where crabs, shrimp and shellfish abound -- pretty much the same as school sized weaks. Both species will move around a good deal, though, and finding them one day is no guarantee that you've got them figured out. One way to quickly locate these fish if they are not where you found them last is to drift behind or downtide of a commercial clam dredge. As they work, these boats dig up the bottom, exposing shellfish, crabs and worms in effect creating a giant chum slick. A second method is to create your own chum slick with crushed mussel or skimmer clam a la flounder chumming.

Rest assured, the term weakfish does not refer to either fish's fighting ability. Both are strong fighters capable of making powerful, fast runs, especially if played on light tackle. Instead, the weak in weakfish points to the delicate mouth tissue of these trout-like finsters. As many a heart-broken fisherman will tell you after dropping a large weak or sea trout in the middle of a fight, this tissue tears all too easily allowing hooks to rip free when too much pressure is exerted on the line.

Unlike bluefishing, where a tight drag and brute strength often prevail, sea trout and weakfishermen must use all their angling skills to seduce, outwit, and whip a lunker. Proper attention must be paid to drag setting, knots, line and every other aspect of tackle. Most importantly, play these fish gently, just as you would a freshwater trout taken on light line.

Large weakfish are often referred to as tiderunners. This reflects the tendency of the larger weaks to move in and out of inlets and bays on moving water. Fish of less than three pounds are called schoolies or spikes and are frequently taken by porgy fishermen using high-low rigs baited with squid strips, shrimp, peeler crabs or sandworms. Anything in between is simply called a weak or sea trout. Spring-run tiderunners are usually taken while drift fishing, while summer schoolies or spotted sea trout more often fall to anchored boaters.

The standard lure for spring tiderunners today is the nine inch jellyworm. These are threaded onto any of a variety of leadheads and dragged along the bottom, as is or with the addition of a sandworm or pennant of squid. Use the lightest weight head that will allow you to keep contact with the bottom. They should be worked slowly with occasional slight twitches imparted by *gently* lifting your rod tip three or four inches. During daylight hours, the preferred color is strawberry, but after dark many veterans switch over to bright white. Keep in mind, however, that color preference may change from season to season or even day to day. Since sea trout tend to run a little smaller than the weaks, you might want to try a smaller worm, say six inches, in areas where that species predominates.

Until a few years ago, the hot ticket to weakfish and sea trout scores was plastic or rubber shrimp imitations such as Bagley's Salty Dog. While these have taken a backseat of late to jellyworms and surge tube lures, they are still occasionally productive when given half a chance. Pink has always been my most productive color, but many anglers swear by green, amber, or white. These imitation shrimp are fished in the same manner as are the jellyworms, with or without an addition.

Of course, bucktails still work on weakfish and sea trout; they always have and always will. White or yellow bucktails in the one to three ounce range, tipped with squid and hopped off the bottom with slightly more enthusiasm than the jellyworms, are always a good bet. Whiptails, Nordic Eels or other surge tube lures are usually worked in a similar manner. (Surge tube lures may also be trolled on umbrella rigs to take deep holding weaks when all else fails. In fact, the weak is often taken accidently this way by anglers looking for stripers and bluefish, especially in rip or inlet waters.)

Finally, in the realm of lures, the diamond jig certainly has a place in the hearts (or mouths) of weakfish. Many times weaks can be jigged in deep water by working lures slowly just above the bottom. The standard procedure is to allow the jig to settle to the bottom and then crank it at a slow to medium pace for five or six turns. If you do not hook up, repeat the process. This method is especially productive in the waters of Long Island Sound and New York Bight where the weaks like to cruise beneath large schools of bluefish, eating the scraps which sink to the bottom as the choppers rip into a school of baitfish. In this situation, your appointed task is to make the jig appear to be a maimed baitfish struggling to regain its balance.

Although lures are often used to take tiderunner weakfish, baitfishing can be productive, too. A small spot, mullet, bunker, grunt or snapper blue can be impaled on a 2/0 beak, a sproat style hook, or a fish finder rig and trailed behind a drifting boat to take the largest of these gamefish. For sinker bouncers, a large squid strip, shrimp or whole sandworm can be strung on a 1/0 to 3/0 beak (baitholder) style hook and allowed to free spool into the current with a split shot or two to help keep it down. When school weaks abound, as sometimes happens in the midst of porgy fishing, a high-low rig can even be used. The bottom hook is baited with the usual porgy bait while the high hook is set out with a long pennant of squid, a strip bait (snapper or spot work best) or a sandworm. In more southerly waters, where porgies are less abundant, shrimp, peeler crabs or squid strips are often used on both hooks

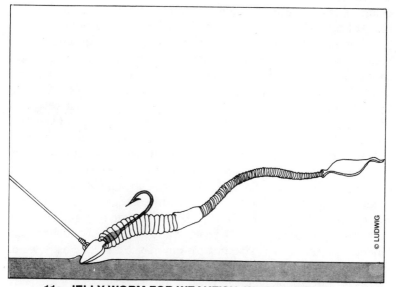

11a. JELLY WORM FOR WEAKFISH. Worked right on the bottom, these account for many tiderunner weaks. They can be used plain or tipped with a whole sandworm or a strip of squid.

with sea trout and kingfish (northern whiting) the main objectives.

No matter what the bait, I find that most weakfish pick up an offering lightly, although on occasion a fish does set the hook on itself with a jolting strike. Generally, though, pickups are gentle and many novice fishermen never even know that they have been hit. At the first indication of a strike, I usually lower my rod tip toward the water and wait for the slack in the line to tighten on its own before setting the hook. This gives the fish a split second to get the bait or lure fully into its mouth but not enough time to distinguish the hook. As the line tightens, set the hook hard, for although the weakfish has a mouth which tears easily a fair amount of pressure is required to pierce the skin of a tiderunner.

Due to the tender mouths and strong fighting ability of weakfish and sea trout, the tackle used to do battle must have a little give. As such, spinning gear is the ideal choice for these species. A reel capable of handling between 6 and 15 lb. test line should be matched to a six to seven foot rod. Choose a rod which is fast tapered but still has some decent backbone. Such a rod will give at the top when the fish suddenly lunges, but will also have the strength to wear down a weak on the run. A light baitcasting or conventional setup capable of handling the same strength lines and with a rod possessing similar qualities will, of course, work well too. Regardless of which setup you employ, be sure to choose a reel with a smooth drag. Drags which do not function properly or are not correctly set account for more lost weaks than any other factor. It should be noted here that most party boats leave a lot to be desired when rental tackle for weakfish is concerned. Often, the rods are too stiff, drags are not quite smooth enough, and lines are a little too heavy, so it pays to bring your own equipment on these trips.

Upon realizing that it has been duped, most weakfish and sea trout respond with a powerful first run followed by two or three runs of shorter duration. It is on this first run that many fish are lost as excited fishermen panic or drags too tightly set cause the hook to rip free. Take your time when playing one of these beauties and let your rod and drag combine to tire out the fish. That first big run may last as long as 30 yards (although it is often much shorter), but those who maintain their cool and resist the temptation to crank while the fish is stripping line against the drag more often than not win the battle.

Be certain the fish is dead tired before bringing it alongside the boat since a green fish will likely make one last ditch dive at boatside, pos-

Large weakfish are great eating as well as a great challenge. Here a fine specimen is securely in the net.

sibly tangling lines and tearing free of the hook in the process. If all goes well, you'll slip the net under the fish with relative ease and you can then stand back and admire your accomplishment in whipping one of the cagiest and most handsome fish in our waters -- regardless of which of these two cousins you've managed to deck.

Chapter 12

⚓

Fluke
(Summer Flounder)

Usually taken on the drift, fluke or summer flounder are most abundant when water temperatures are between 65 to 70 degrees. Second only to bluefish in popularity among east coast small boat anglers, this fine tasting treat is prized by both commercial and recreational fishermen with average landings over the past several years holding steady at about 60 million pounds, split almost equally between the two interests.

Best distinguished from its close cousin the winter flounder by larger average size and a set of sturdy dentures, fluke are bottom dwelling predators with a passion for small baitfish. As such, they gravitate toward generally turbulent waters where shiners, sandeels, small snappers, baby bunker or other finned food sources are easily disoriented by swirling currents. Favored haunts include inlets, channels that crisscross sheltered bay or sound waters, the downtide side of a sandbar, dock or wreck, and open ocean rips in depths of 20 to 60 feet. Of course, with so many location types capable of holding fish, the dilemma becomes choosing the right tackle to get the job done, for although the methodology of fluke fishing is basically the same in each area, the differing conditions make for wide disparity in ideal setups.

For working bay or small inlet waters where the currents are not too intense and water depth is not likely to exceed 20 feet or so, a fairly limber five and a half to seven foot rod and matching baitcasting or spin-

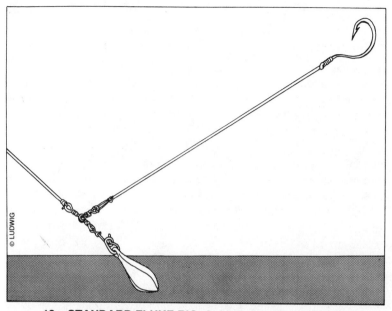

12a. STANDARD FLUKE RIG. A dropper loop can be used in place of the 3-way swivel.

© LUDWIG

ning reel filled with 8 to 12 pound test line is what the doctor prescribes. In such waters, only two to three ounces of weight will be needed to hold bottom and the majority of fluke encountered will weigh less than three pounds with a four to six pound fish reason for a great, big smile. It is this type of fluke action most anglers are familiar with and it is in such shallow areas that thrill-seekers can also try for line class records with ultra-light tackle in the two to six pound category.

For those intent on catching a few fish, not breaking lines or records, single hook bottom rigs with a 30 to 36 inch length of 30 lb. test leader and 1/0 or 2/0 Carlisle or sproat style hook are the usual choice. My personal preference, however, is for a 2/0 wide gap style hook and an 18 to 24 inch leader. I feel that these hooks dig in and hold flatfish much better than other styles and, as a result, less fish shake free while I'm trying to get the net in the water. The shorter leader allows me more control over the action I try to impart to my baits. The hooks, by the way, should be tied into the main line about four inches above the sinker.

When fishing the open ocean, swift moving water deeper than 20 feet, or locations with strong currents, a little heavier tackle and rigging becomes necessary. Success in these situations often hinges on the

ability to hold bottom. To accomplish this task, gutsy 3/0 conventional style reels and fairly stiff rods measuring between five and six and a
half feet in length are more in order. Lines should test between 20 and
30 lbs. Spinning gear in the 17 to 20 lb. class can also be used in this
kind of water, but it's a poor second choice.

The typical terminal rig employed when fishing turbulent inlet or
ocean waters consists of a 36 inch length of 30 to 40 lb. test leader
material snelled to a 2/0 to 4/0 Carlisle hook. This rig is tied to the
main line via a dropper loop approximately two to six inches above a
four to eight ounce bank sinker. Many anglers use a three-way swivel
and sinker snap in place of the dropper loop. As with inshore fluking,
I often substitute a wide gap style hook (size 2/0 to 4/0) and slightly
shorter length of leader. Some anglers use pre-tied rigs adorned with
larger spinner blades and surgical tubing. These are frequently used for
shallow water fluking too. While these rigs do have their days, I tend to
shy away from them because they catch a lot of grass. Remember the
#1 rule of bottom fishing: Use as little hardware as you can get away
with! The less hardware you use, the less chance of it catching grass,
snagging or having a connection just give out.

Like tackle, bait selection also varies depending on whether you fish
bay or ocean waters. For bay fishing, standard baits include live killies,
frozen spearing, or frozen sand eels. A whole baitfish is teamed on one
hook with a single strip of squid and the entire concoction is called "a
ham and eggs" combo. There are several advantages to using such combination baits when fluke fishing. It gives the fish a chance to strike at
either offering, allows the dark baitfish to show up against sandy bottoms and the white strip of squid to show clearly against mud bottoms,
and gives the fisherman a "second chance" should one piece of bait un-
knowingly fall off the hook or be stripped by a fish.

To prepare a ham and eggs combo, hook a single strip of squid once
through the middle of the widest end. Leave the barb exposed and make
sure that the squid strip hangs straight down from the bend of the hook.
Make the strip a quarter to one half inch wide by three to five inches
long. If fishing with frozen bait such as sand eels, place a single baitfish
over the squid strip by passing the hook through one eye and out the
other. Leave the barb exposed. When using live bait such as killies, carefully thread the hook through the mouth and out the gill. Leave the barb
exposed at the top of the gill cover with the point facing up. Whichever
bait you use keep in mind that fluke are bottom feeders, much like

flounder, and so your bait should always be worked as close to the sea floor as possible.

Sometimes, fluke seem intent on committing suicide and really rap these baits. On these days, which are not all that common, set the hook as soon as you feel the strike. Most of the time, however, fluke will signal their pickup with one or two medium strength taps, enough to let you know they are there but not enough to convince you that they have swallowed the bait. The proper response to these fish is to lower your rod tip toward the water to create a little slack line and wait a second until the boat's drift tightens the line again. At this point you should feel a slight heaviness or dragging at the end of your line. Rather than set the hook immediately, slowly lift your rod tip until it's at about a 45 degree angle with the water. This will lift the fluke a little off the bottom but still allow it to keep a firm grasp on the bait. The fluke will not stand for being off the bottom for more than a few seconds and will eventually decide to dive -- setting the hook on itself! (This is similar to the "slow lift method" described in the section on winter flounder.) Set the hook yourself just to make sure it's in solid. If the fish is still holding the bait by the time you raise the rod tip to 45 degrees, but does not dive for the bottom, set the hook and pray. You'll find that when the fish are in a finicky mood, you'll drop as many as you hook with this method but it's the most consistent way of hooking flatfish I've come across so far.

On occasion, when baitfish (especially small snappers or silversides) are plentiful and water temperatures not too hot during early or mid-summer, pods of fluke may move up onto shallow flats to feed. If clouds obscure the sun for two or three days and boat traffic is somewhat quiet, the fish may feel comfortable with as little as three feet of water over their heads. When this happens, its possible to catch them using a float rig. Simply tie a 1/0 sproat or wide gap style hook to a 30" length of 20 lb. test leader and attach this to the end of your line with a clinch knot. Now secure a float three to five feet above the hook. No sinkers are used although two or three split shots should be pinched about mid-way up the leader.

Once the rigging is complete, impale a live killie or small (three to four inch) snapper as previously described, toss your line thirty to fifty feet behind the boat and place your pole in a rod holder. Keep the bail closed. As the boat drifts over the flats, your offering will be towed along. If you've placed the float at the right height, the split shots should keep the bait within six inches to a foot of the sea floor but out of the reach

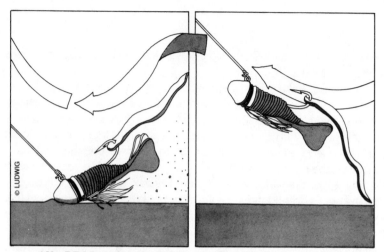

12b. DEADLY FLUKE COMBO: LEAD HEAD AND SQUID STRIP.

of annoying crabs and hackleheads. Also, because there is no sinker dragging across the bottom there should be little trouble with weeds, even in areas where eel grass grows in scattered matts. When a fluke grabs your offering, you'll see the float submerge. Simply pick up the pole and set the hook -- it's that easy. Most of the fish you take with this method will be on the small side, usually in the 14 to 16 inch range, but there are occasional surprises. I've taken several five pounders this way and have seen fish to seven pounds taken in water less than four feet deep! Light spinning tackle is ideal for this shallow water action. Sandy, grassy flats bordering deep channels seem to produce the best.

While drifting with bait is the most popular method of fluking, there is a growing cadre of anglers who find the added excitement of jigging to be a real turn on. On those days when the fish don't seem to be responsive to natural baits, leadhead jigs, bucktails, or soft bodied plastic lures (two to four ounces) such as Smiling Bills, Salty Dogs or Sassy Shads may have that added action that the fish crave -- especially if tipped with a thin strip bait or squid pennant. These lures should be let out far enough from the boat that they hold bottom. Jig them with a slight hopping motion but be sure not to jig too vigorously as you want to keep your bait within about six inches of the bottom at all times.

Jigging often provokes solid strikes and setting the hook is little problem although there are days when the fish sort of suck in the lures. On those tough days, drop your rod tip slowly while keeping a slight tension on the line at all times as you feel that now familiar heaviness.

Instead of lifting your rod tip to 45 degrees as is done when bait fishing, however, the hook should be set as soon as all the slack is out of the line and the rod begins to take on a bend. This gives the fluke a second to get the hook in its mouth but not enough time to decide it isn't fond of plastic, bucktail or feathers. You'll find jigging most apt to out-perform natural baits around slack tides when the added motion and flash can be a real eye-catcher to a fish that's probably already had enough to eat.

Although killies, spearing, or sand eels may also be used in ocean waters, long squid strip and smelt combos or strip baits seem to work better. The reason for the change in baits is fairly simple. The tides and currents in these waters are usually much stronger than inshore and killies and small frozen baits are often torn from the hook by the water as they descend to the bottom. Additionally, ocean fluke tend to run somewhat larger than those in bay waters. The average ocean caught fish runs about two to three pounds with a surprising number between 7 and 12 pounds, and these are more interested in bigger baits. Smelt and squid combos are made in the same way as sand eel or spearing and squid combos. Passing the hook through the eyes of the smelt or through the bottom jaw and out the middle of the skull will keep this bait on the hook whereas the same large hook would likely destroy the small head of the baitfish used in bay fishing.

Paying close attention to the differences between bay and ocean fishing is vitally important to the fluke fanatic, but too many anglers give it only casual thought. I can remember, a few years back, fishing on a party boat ocean excursion for big flatfish. Most of the veteran flukers were using standard bay equipment and having a great deal of difficulty holding bottom and feeling bites in the strong rips we were working. Although the mate had suggested that light spinning gear be put away in favor of free use of conventional outfits, most anglers chose to stay with what they had brought on board. All of a sudden, from about midship, a loud, frantic call rang out. It was almost a plea.

"Net! Net! Where's the mate? This kid's got the pool winner!"

All heads on the port side swung toward midship and the 10-year-old in question as the mate scurried from his perch on the cabin ladder.

"I'm coming! Just keep his head in the water!" hollered the mate as he skipped over a cooler which lay open in the aisle.

From my perch on the bow, I watched in anxious anticipation, leaning over the rail for a better view. From the strain on the mate's face as he lifted the net, I could tell it was big.

Spontaneous cheers and applause erupted around the boat as 12 lbs. of flattie hit the deck with a solid thud. The grin on the young fisherman's face stretched ear to ear and his smile spread like wildfire to most nearby anglers as, in his excitement, the child jumped up and down while shaking every hand he could find.

While smiling, though, most veterans were shaking their heads in disbelief. How lucky could the kid get? He was not only a shoe-in for the pool (displacing a fat four pounder I had decked earlier in the day - - rats!) but he had caught the second highest number of fish for the day.

COURTESY THE JAMAICA, BRIELLE, NJ

A prized doormat fluke taken aboard the New Jersey based Jamaica II, Brielle, NJ.

Strip Baits: A Good Alternative

Strip baits, used alone or as a replacement for squid strips, are one of the most productive fluke enticers in many areas. Made from fillets of fluke or by-catch species such as sea robins, dogfish, sandsharks or snappers, these strips should be cut so that they are long and thin — just as a strip of squid should be. Leave the skin on and trim the meat until it is ¼"-½" thick.

The main advantages of fish vs. squid strips are (1) the skin of the fish strip will keep the bait on your hook longer and, (2) the fluke may be more receptive to it if they have been feeding on the species from which the strip was cut. Strips cut from the back of most species will be dark in color and show up well against sandy bottoms. Strips cut from the belly sections are generally light in color and thus are highly visible to flatfish feeding over mud, rock or other dark colored bottom. As with squid strips, hook each strip once through the wide end. For added action, split the last 2" of the tail. You'll find that strip baits also work well for such species as weakfish, whiting, ling, and bluefish.

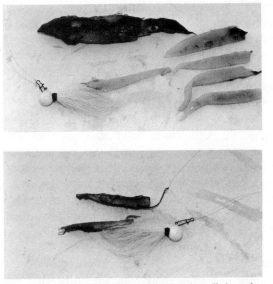

Long tapered strips of squids (top) or fish strips (bottom) work well when used with leadheads.

It was no surprise to the mate, though. He went on to explain to me later that while all the old salts were using their favorite bay rods, the youngster was using a pole and rig supplied by the boat that was better suited to the fishing conditions. He also mimicked the way the mate had showed him of baiting the hook and working the rod tip. Because of this, he had no trouble holding bottom or feeling sensitive bites. It was this youngster's eagerness to learn and willingness to listen that earned him such great rewards.

And isn't that the beauty of fishing? Anyone willing to listen and learn can get in on the action. Oh sure, there are always going to be naturals -- the guy who catches 30 blackfish or decks 10 fluke on his first trip but more often than not, it's those fishermen who put in their time on the water, really fish hard while they're out, and listen to the advice of more experienced anglers who will bring home the fillets. Simple determination and a desire to learn are the prime ingredients for success in any fishing situation.

Because the baits and hooks used when working ocean rips are much larger than those used in more protected areas, anglers sometimes resort to a slip sinker rig. When a bite is registered on this rig, the angler disengages the reel and allows 10 to 20 feet of line to free-spool into the current before re-engaging. When the line comes tight, the rod is slowly lifted to 45 degrees and the hook set as described earlier. When used with the proper hooks, this rig is deadly on flounder too.

No discussion on fluke fishing would be complete without a brief mention of live snappers and baby bunker as bait. Small snappers (baby blues) three to five inches long can be fished dead or alive in bay waters on the same rigs used to work ham and egg combos. Slightly larger specimens, however, account for some of the heftiest fluke taken each season, especially at the inlets or in ocean rips. In fact, among accomplished anglers it's common knowledge that these two baits in the six to eight inch size probably account for close to 75% of all doormat (eight pounds plus) sized fluke taken. Both the snappers and bunker require large amounts of oxygen so you'll need an aerated live well to keep them from dying. For ocean fishing, these livebaits are best worked on the slip sinker rig previously described. Either bait can be hooked through the nostrils, just in front of the dorsal fin, or through the lips. If you want, a stinger hook can be added and positioned at the tail. A twenty to forty foot drop- back when a hit is felt should allow the predator to injest your offering deep enough to make hook setting bet-

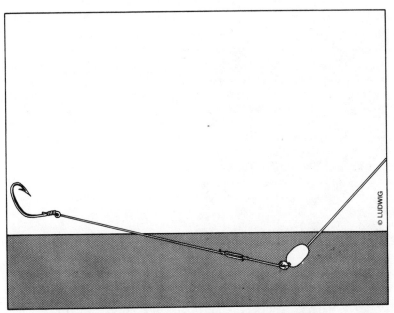

12c. SLIP SINKER RIG FOR FLUKE OR FLOUNDER.

ter than a 50/50 proposition. With the stinger, you can set the hook right away, but I find the hits less frequent with this rig and so I usually take the single hook route.

When using snappers or bunker, its a given that some are going to die before they're ever put on a hook. Don't throw away those that die, because the next best bait for doormat fluke (after big, live baitfish) are big strip baits and both snappers and bunker are excellent for this purpose.

When is the best time to try for a doormat sized fluke? Charlie Nappie, world record holder with a 22 pound 7 ounce whopper and several smaller line class records to his credit, feels the answer is the last 15 minutes of any tide. According to Nappie, at these times the waters are moving fast enough to continue tossing baitfish around, but most of the smaller, more aggressive fluke have already eaten their fill. Thus, those baitfish still in trouble are easy pickings for the biggest, oldest and laziest of summer flatties. Look for the biggest fluke to come from the most turbulent rips.

No matter where you dunk a bait, fluke are netted. Unfortunately, they look so helpless at the end of a line that anglers often try to swing them over the rail. Quite a few fish are lost this way, especially large

Shiners and sandeels are favored baits for fluke of all sizes. You can assure yourself of having fresh bait by seining your own.

ones. If you find yourself with the fish at the rail and a wait for the net, just keep steady pressure on the line and the fluke should swim right alongside the boat without putting up too much resistance. Lift its head out of the water, though, and it's as good as gone -- and nobody wants to lose a keeping sized fluke as these fish are as good as flounder when it comes to suppertime.

One last thought: Remember to always set your drag properly prior to starting out, and check it from time to time to be sure the tension has not changed. Fluke of doormat proportions will quite readily take line while making short, dogged runs and can easily pop a line that doesn't give because the drag is locked down tight.

Chapter 13

⚓

Porgies And Seabass

Although quite different in appearance, these two delights are frequently mentioned in tandem. The reason for this connection is simple: porgies and black seabass commonly inhabit the same types of bottom, feed on similar foods, and so are often caught together. For the sake of convenience I'm going to break these two apart for a few paragraphs and discuss each in detail. But be assured that these sweet tasting critters often share the headlines of late summer, especially north of Delaware Bay.

Growing up on Long Island, where the porgy or scup was a mainstay of the east end fleet, I came to know the months of August and September as "Porgy Time!". Although I was always curious about catching these silver sided panfish, it wasn't until I was about 20 years of age that I first boarded a party boat with scup in mind. What with bluefish and fluke in peak season, why bother to go for smaller stuff? Too bad I waited so long because these pugnacious little creatures offered me one of the most enjoyable and fulfilling trips I have ever taken. The action was red hot most of the day, with a slight lull around the tide change. Before lunch, most anglers were already loading their second bucket with three-quarter pound to two pound fish. What a blast! There were no thrilling battles to be won, no drags screaming with racing fish threatening to snap a taut and straining line, no fish worthy of a special photograph -- just action and plenty of it. It sort of made me feel like a little kid again.

At top, a typical fall porgy—about three-fourths of a pound. At left, a porgy taken off the Connecticut coast. Note the heavy spinning gear.

TINA SCHLICHTER

Inshore bottom fishing for porgies is ideal for beginning anglers as this species is usually abundant (catches are sometimes measured by the bucketful), only marginally difficult to hook, and excellent tablefare. They require nothing out of the ordinary in the tackle and bait departments and although highly spirited for their size, can easily be tamed by a 10-year-old. Because these fish are such easy pickings on most days, few frayed tempers are found among the fishermen and lots of good natured ribbing is the general rule between anglers or even neighboring boats. Since porgies frequently inhabit shallow water areas, they are favorites of private and rental boaters, replacing winter flounder as a fishing option once waters achieve summertime temperatures. Of course, being plentiful and good eating, porgies are also frequently targeted by the charter and party boat fleets.

Most active when water temperatures are between 60 to 65 degrees, the porgy sports a silver hue along its sides with purple, olive, or bronze highlights on the back and a white or silver underside. Due to its body shape, it can make sharp turns in tight quarters, resulting in a herky-jerky type battle when hooked. Its long pelvic fins, placed forward, aid in braking while sharp spines on the dorsal fins help to keep hungry predators at bay. Occasionally, these spines may pierce the skin of a careless fisherman. Porgies have a steep profile and a small pointy mouth loaded with tiny teeth (harmless to you and me) which they use to pick small crabs, mollusks, and minnows off the bottom. Most of their summers are spent in northern waters from New Jersey to Massachusetts where they set up in the vicinity of mussel beds, wrecks and rockpiles, especially when these structures are bordered by clean, sand bottoms. Occasionally, the smallest porgies, often called sand porgies, will take residence along sandy beaches offering fast sport for shorebound children. During the winter months, the fish migrate to deepwater offshore spawning grounds south of the Virginia or Carolina coasts.

Primarily a bottom feeder and most fond of munching during a moving tide, porgies will rise a foot or two from home base to examine an interesting bait lowered from an anchored boat. These tight schooling critters enjoy a well earned reputation as bait stealers, but their vast numbers virtually assure that even the neophyte angler will head home with a sack full of fish on any given day. Because they school tightly, porgies are highly susceptible to chumming. Thus, it should come as no surprise that a pot full of crushed mussels or ground clam worked vigorously on the bottom every five minutes or so will increase your daily scores substantially. Most porgies weigh in at less than a pound, but during the fall run and on select grounds such as the Nantucket Shoals off of Massachusetts, or Block Island Sound, they may average larger and run upwards of four pounds. These two locations are a ways offshore, though, and are usually worked by the party boat fleet or large private craft. For the inshore angler, a true two pound porgy is one for the photo album.

The tackle you choose to porgy fish with must reflect the conditions of the location in which you fish. Party boaters working the Nantucket Shoals, for instance, will need conventional setups and 20 to 30 lb. test lines because of strong tides and deep water. On the other hand, those who fish in New Jersey bays or the west end of Long Island Sound may at times get away with spinning gear, 6 to 12 pound test line and one to three ounce bank sinkers. Whenever possible, I prefer to fish in water that allows the use of the lighter gear.

Part scavenger, part predator, porgies are voracious feeders. Given the chance, they will consume shellfish (skimmer clam, sea worms or squid strips are the usual offering), sand or blood worms, small minnows, fiddler crab, shrimp and even small fish strips. Although they can also be taken on small jigs and leadheads, few anglers bother to work lures for this species, save for an occasional small surgical tube tied a foot above the top hook on some rigs.

A pair of size #4 or #6 gold beak style baitholder hooks with barbed shanks to help hold the bait in place are generally used for small porgies; size #2 or #1 are favored for the jumbos and humpbacks. In either case, the hooks should be snelled to 12 inch leaders of 20 to 30 lb. test and tied tandem style. For large porgies, a hi-low rig with the top hook approximately 15 inches off the bottom can be substituted. Sinker weights will vary, of course, depending on where one fishes.

Porgies are quick striking fish, so maintaining a tight line at all times is essential to detecting their bites. Usually, their interest is signaled by a series of rapid, light taps, followed by a sharp rap. Set the hook immediately following that last rap for if you wait a second too long, you'll be retrieving a bare hook from the water.

Once hooked, porgies take off on a series of short, high speed darts with plenty of direction changes. If you are using one of the two-hook rigs described above, it's a good idea to let that fish circle around on the bottom for a few seconds as you keep a tight line. Other fish in the school, attracted by all the commotion, will undoubtedly attempt to pick the bait off the free hook, resulting in an occasional double header.

ext to bluefish, I can't think of another coastal species that has more nicknames than the porgy. As with the larger blue, the names given to this panfish usually are descriptive of it's size. The smallest fish, usual-

Next to bluefish, I can't think of another coastal species that has more nicknames than the porgy. As with the larger blue, the names given to this panfish usually are descriptive of it's size. The smallest fish, usual-

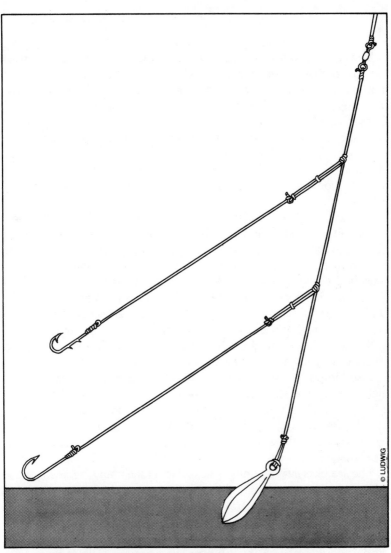

13a. HIGH-LOW RIG FOR PORGIES OR SEABASS.

ly less than half a pound, are called sand porgies. Porgie, scup, or mediums are names used to describe fish of three-quarters to a pound and a half. Jumbos are porgies of a pound and a half to about two pounds and anything larger is proudly referred to as a humpback, a name whose origin will be evident should you be fortunate enough to examine such a trophy.

The black seabass is a beautiful looking fish of exceptional quality on the dinner plate. Less abundant and slightly more structure oriented than is the porgy, this irredescently-hued finster is found along the coast from Maine to Florida but is most highly concentrated in Delaware and Chesapeake Bays and along the New Jersey, New York and Connecticut shores. Varied body markings give the sea bass a spotty appearance. The back is usually dark brown or black with occasional indigo and blue hues, while the belly is checkered white or grey. They are most at home when water temperatures range between 65 to 70 degrees.

Bay sea bass (pin bass) generally run one pound or less while ocean fish tend to be a little larger. Both sizes, however, prefer hard, sandy, obstructed bottoms, and so they often mix with porgies over wrecks or shellfish beds. They live offshore during the winter months but invade shallow coastal regions in late May or June, frequently setting up shop in late summer around the base of bridge abutments and inlet jetties. During their fall migration back offshore, sea bass school tightly over broken bottom and become highly susceptible to the baited hook. It is at this time that most of the larger bass, three to five pounders, are taken, usually from ocean waters.

Like the porgy, sea bass can be caught on a variety of baits. Skimmer clam or squid strips are again the most often employed but live killies, blood worms, squid heads, and shedder or fiddler crabs are often used by veteran anglers. A few sports jig them up, but this can get to be expensive as the structure in which these battlers reside can eat a great many lures.

The sea bass lives an unusual sexual life. Like many members of the *Serranidae* (grouper) family, they are protogynous hermaphrodites and sexually dimorphic. In fisherman's terms, this means that small fish are usually lassies but turn into lads sometime after their seventh birthday. At this time, they begin to develop humped backs, facial stripes and territorial aggressiveness. Any fish over five pounds is likely to be a male.

Since sea bass are often a by-catch of porgy and tog fishermen (north of New Jersey), the tackle used to take them is usually dictated by the more prevalent species. Thus, rigs used when sea bass are in town are slightly altered porgy setups. It's best to use the high-low rig and make the top choice a beak or sproat style hook. The bottom point is usually a Virginia but could also be an O'Shaughnessy or Carlisle. I tend to opt for the beak on top unless blackfish are mixed with the bass and porgies. In this case I'll use Virginia top and bottom. For bay fishing, a size 1/0 hook will suffice but ocean action requires a 2/0 to 3/0 hook in case you run into any humpbacked three pound plus bass.

Because most sea bass and porgy fishing takes place while anchored over wrecks or other bottom structure, you'll find some surprising incidentals mixing in these catches from time to time. Would you believe that, aside from the expected blackfish, I've taken fluke, ling, cod, skates, sculpin, and mackerel while porgy fishing. Other anglers report landing sting rays (up to 100 lbs.), striped bass, monster bluefish, pollack, and huge trigger fish. If you believe that variety is the spice of life, then this kind of fishing trip is for you.

By the way, you'll find that the one to two pound sea bass which frequent bay waters take a bait differently than their larger brethren. The former are prone to taste and nibble your baits before committing, while the latter simply gulp down whatever seems appealing. These larger fish will give an excellent account of themselves on any suitable tackle. And, since there's more to them, they'll give an even better account of themselves on the dinner plate.

PETE BARRETT

Chapter 14

⚓

Whiting And Ling

Few souls are adventurous, brave, or foolhardy enough to venture forth from a warm house and a good basketball game during the dead of winter, but for those who do, whiting and ling offer the promise of full sacks and some downright tasty meals. Especially populous in the waters of the New York Bight, catches of these cold water predators are often measured by the pailful once the season swings into high gear.

As with codfish, whiting and ling are most frequently taken from party boats. One reason is that they seldom move in real close. Another is the often brutal winter weather they're taken during. Whiting and ling inshore migrations reach their peak somewhere between late November and early January. Yet, even though it is called an inshore migration, these species rarely enter bay or sound waters. In fact, the vast majority of whiting and ling are pulled up from 60 to 180 foot depths. This is usually a bit out of range for the small boater, especially during winter-time. While this kind of fishing could prove brutal on a small boat, party boats, with their heated handrails and cozy cabins, are well suited to such action. Even on a party boat, however, the most important concern is dressing properly for the weather. To that end, a hat, waterproof gloves, boots and several layers of warm clothing will be as important as what bait you use.

This pair always reminds me of those old comedy routines like Laurel and Hardy or Abbott and Costello, for the whiting is long, lean and sharp in appearance while his counterpart the ling qualifies for the adjectives short and dumpy. For more tangible reasons, it will be necessary to separate the two, at least for a few paragraphs.

Our friend the whiting is in actuality a silver hake but few fishermen use that name when discussing this aggressive feeder. In some locales they are known as frostfish because in the dead of winter, after moving into shallow water, they sometimes get so caught up in their relentless pursuit of baitfish that they chase their prey right up onto the beach where they can be easily speared or even gathered by hand. At one time this was considered popular sport, especially in the vicinity of Coney Island, New York and Long Beach, N.J. But it seems that the fish have not been as prone to sacrifice themselves in recent years, probably due to an overall decrease in population. I imagine, though, that there are still a few oldtimers who know when the time is right to go "pickin'" at the beach.

Long and slender with a brownish topside fading to silver underneath, the whiting is unique in shape, roughly comparable to a little league style baseball bat. Although they can attain weights of several pounds, a three pounder is considered large with the average usually running between three-quarters and two pounds.

A dark and ugly fish, the ling (red hake) looks something like a cross between a cod and an eel. Strictly a bottom dweller, ling have been known to reach weights up to 30 lbs., but I'd say that the average for rod and reel caught fish is between one and three pounds with a four to five pounder virtually guaranteeing the pool for the day.

Double, triple, and even quadruple hook bottom rigs are standard fare when playing the whiting and ling game. Most of the season, you shouldn't need more than a 3/0 reel spooled with a good length of 30 pound test mono or dacron, and a stout rod capable of handling weights in the six to ten ounce range. During the dead of winter and at the beginning or end of the season the fish may be found in water depths of 180 to 250 feet, and at these times a 4/0 reel and stiff rod that can handle 12 to 16 ounces of lead may prove a better choice. Assuming you'll catch most of these fish while party boating, it's always a good idea to call ahead and find out how deep the fish are feeding before heading out.

As far as hook choice is concerned, both ling and whiting have fair sized mouths so there is some leeway. A 2/0 to 4/0 O'Shaughnessy or Sproat serves the purpose for most anglers. Some prefer long shanked Kirby or Carlisle styles because the whiting has a fair set of dentures and the long shanks make unhooking easier.

Keep in mind when tying your rigs that, although whiting may feed several feet off the bottom, ling are strictly cellar dwellers. Because of this, you will always want at least one hook only four to five inches above your sinker. (Remember too, ling cop the pool money on most party boat trips). My favorite rig for whiting/ling consists of a 4/0 sproat style bottom hook tied into a four foot length of 30 pound test mono leader via a dropper loop four inches above my sinker; a second 4/0 sproat 18 inches above the bottom hook; and a small green or red tube lure roughly 20 inches above the top hook. The bottom two hooks are baited with fresh whiting strip baits while the tube lure is left unadorned. This rig presents the fish with the option of tubes or bait at three different levels. If I notice a pattern in my catches, such as all the fish taking the tube, I simply tie up a new rig and use whatever the fish seem to prefer. If the fish all hit only the top hook, I might take out the middle hook and put it higher on the rig, leaving the bottom hook where it is in case a stray ling happens by.

Bait poses little problem when fishing for this dynamic duo. Most party boats supply skimmer clam, strips of herring or strips of whiting from the previous day's catch. You'll fare better, though, if you can force yourself to sacrifice your first whiting or two of the day to make fresh strip baits. Strips cut from the silvery belly section are especially productive. The baits supplied by the boats are usually frozen and thus tend to pull off the hook rather easily. A fresh strip stays on real well and may even last through several fish. Just be sure to change your baits whenever they get frazzled. As always, hook the strip bait once in the widest end. (See the section on fluke for more on strip baits).

Whiting and ling can be taken at anchor or on the drift. They are also taken both day and night. In fact, some ports have party boats sailing at 7 P.M. or later -- despite the chill of winter evenings. Since whiting school tightly, drifting tends to produce spurts of activity as the boat passes over separate schools of fish. At these times you will find that letting a fish struggle at the end of your line for a minute or two after setting the hook may produce multiple hookups. This can work when the boat is anchored as well. Drifting seems to cut down considerably on the number of ling taken. There are two reasons for this: First, ling tend to stay close to wrecks and drifting only puts your lines over the obstruction for a limited amount of time; and second, it's a little harder

Warm coats with hoods are the order of the day for this cold weather fishing. Here, two whiting have just come over the rail.

to keep your line right on the bottom when drifting so whiting are more apt to see your hooks than are the ling.

Anchoring is usually done over some sort of bottom structure such as a wreck, underwater hump, or ledge, and a good set of loran numbers are essential for private boat renegades. Fishing at anchor usually entails a brief flurry of action during the first half hour or so followed by a steady pick along the rail. While whiting are still the most prevalent, a fair number of ling should mix in here. If the boat has been drifting for most of the day and the skipper decides to anchor, make sure that bottom hook is in place and well baited because this time will probably be your best chance to win the pool.

Most days, whiting and ling like their baits to be jigged with a fair amount of gusto. Yet there are times, especially during periods of frigid weather, when only a little action needs to be imparted to your line. Both ling and whiting strike with rapid taps -- sort of like a big bergall. Since these fish are usually overmatched by the tackle used, not much muscle needs to be put into setting the hook. For similar reasons, whiting and ling should be reeled to the surface with a steady, medium speed retrieve. Cranking them from the bottom at trans-warp speeds will simply tear the hook from their mouths. Better to bring them in at sub-light.

Although ling are strictly ocean wreck fish, whiting in recent years have been putting in brief appearances within a mile of several New York and New Jersey inlets. At these times it has been possible for private boaters to get in on the action without taking the beating that surely awaits on a longer winter trip. Some of these boaters have reported good success using scaled down rigs and baitcasting poles more attuned to weakfishing. If you find yourself on a private craft with whiting on the prowl, you might want to give such a setup a shot. It might even be possible to take these fish on single hook rigs and six or eight pound test lines. I think it a good bet that they would put up a decent battle on such tackle.

As things stand, though, due to the heavy tackle normally used to catch these one to four pound fish, neither whiting nor ling will ever win a blue ribbon in the fighting department. They do shine brightly in the eats department and can be pan fried, broiled, baked, or even smoked. After eating a few of these fillets, you probably won't care how well they fight, just how fast they fill up a bucket.

Chapter 15

⚓

Codfish

Although many fish are more plentiful, some fight harder and one or two even taste better, no fish pursued by local bottom bouncers holds the allure that cod hold for me. Just the thought that every time I set the hook it might be a 40 to 50 lb. grandaddy at the end of my line really gets my adrenalin flowing. What's more, quite a few interesting incidentals are caught while codfishing, many of them good eating and some of them even larger than the biggest cod!

The winter king! That's how he's known in the southern reaches of his domain. But from Block Island north, this species can be taken right through the summer months provided the boats work in fairly deep water. Cod feed most actively when water temperatures are between 40 to 50 degrees. They can be taken on the drift or at anchor, over wrecks or open bottom. The method employed depends on whether jigging or bait fishing will be the primary means of the day. South of Block Island, the season generally runs from November through early May. In the nothern extent of its range, from Massachusetts through Maine, cod can be caught throughout the year and, at times, even from small boats working inshore waters such as Quincy Bay. Known as "market cod", these inshore fish are generally small, ranging in size from 3 to 12 pounds although a few will undoubtedly push the scales past the 20 lb. mark from time to time. Even up north however, the cows tend to hold in deeper, offshore waters and it's a safe bet that the majority of the catch comes from distant hotspots. At many ports, the trip to favored grounds runs one to two and a half hours. Because the ride to the fish is so long, fares for party and charter boat codfishing are usually quite high, reflecting the amount of gas the boats must spend to get to the fish. You can expect to spend from $28 to $40 for a party boat cod trip. Charter boaters can expect to pay for a full day's offshore action, between $250 and $350. For the private boater looking for off-shore cod action, plenty of anchor line and a good set of loran numbers are a must.

Despite the high price and long trips, the codfish has a loyal and regular following for it offers bottom fishermen their best shot at decking a really large fish. Most party boat trips see at least a couple of 20 pounders, and 30 to 40 pound fish consistently win the pool at some locations. Each season also produces a fair number of soakers in the 40 to 50 pound class with the biggest couple of fish pushing the scale slightly past the 60 lb. mark. Every once in a while a line class world record cod is taken from a party boat, for example Ann Houseknecht's 30 pound class cod of 63.2 pounds taken aboard the Viking Starship of Montauk, NY. World records can be set for incidental species on these trips as well. For example, the Bunny Clark, which sails from Perkins Cove in Ogunquit, Maine, has set line class world records for cod, pollock, and hake.

During the mid-1970's, cod stocks hit an alarming low, especially in the waters south of Massachusetts. The passage of the Fisheries Management Act Of 1970 (200 Mile Limit) gave the stocks a quick breather, and for a while it appeared that populations of Mr. Whiskers were once again on the rise. Unfortunately, heavy pressure from our own commercial fleet has not allowed the fishing to rebound as well as expected, and recent surveys have indicated a noticeable decrease in cod biomass even in the traditionally stable waters north of Mas-sachusetts. Still, it is reasonable for anglers at most ports to expect catches of half a dozen or so fish in the 3 to 20 pound class on any given trip. Average catches may be somewhat less for anglers sailing west and south of Pt. Judith, RI.

Depending on where and when you sail, tackle requirements will vary slightly. Cod can be taken in water as shallow as 40 feet if water temperatures are right. More often they are caught in depths of 160 feet or more. Because of the possibility of hooking into a real lunker and the strong, deep water currents, 4/0 reels spooled with 30 to 40 lb. test and matched to a sturdy six to nine foot rod are the first choice

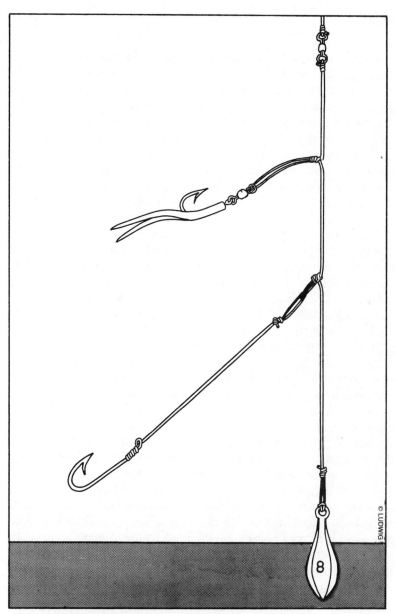

15a. CODFISH RIG WITH TEASER.

of pool sharks. Many anglers, though, manage with 3/0 or 4/0 reels on stout five and a half or six foot rods. In either case, the setup used must be able to handle 8 to 20 ounces of sinker or jig for even if the cod school shallow, they prefer areas with strong running currents.

Rigging for codfish is pretty straightforward. For baitfishing, a 5/0 to 8/0 beak, sproat or O'Shaughnessy style hook is snelled to an 18 to 36 inch leader of 40 or 50 lb. test. This is then tied into the main line via a dropper loop anywhere from 20 to 40 inches above an end loop which is used to secure the bank or diamond sinker. If so desired, a second dropper loop can be tied into the main line a foot or two above the first to attach a surgical tube lure or feather teaser as shown in the drawing. In recent years, a few manufacturers of snelled hooks have experimented with plastic skirts around cod hooks and these seem to be enjoying at least some success. It might be a good idea to give them a try if the opportunity presents itself. Note, too, that some anglers use three-way swivels instead of dropper loops when tying these rigs in the hope of preventing the leader from twisting around the main line. Properly tied, dropper loops will do the job and as you know by now, I like to keep my hardware to a minimum. By the way, since a lot of cod fishing is done over heavy structure, dropping an overhand knot in the line between the hook and sinker as described in the blackfish chapter is always a good idea when dunking bait.

The usual bait is skimmer clam, shrimp, or conch although cod have been known to feed on almost anything that will fit in their mouths including sand eels, herring, strips of haddock, crabs, and worms. In fact before the invention of the aqualung, many new sea shells were discovered when biologists cut open the stomachs of fresh caught cod. Reports of unusual findings in cod autopsies continue to this day with the sole of a shoe, a rubber glove (no hand), a wrist-watch and a man's wallet among some of the more unusual claims. One N.Y. angler even reported finding a set of false teeth in the belly of a cod!

While many novice anglers pile great globs of clam on their hooks in the hope of catching the eye of a huge fish, most old salts will agree that a single skimmer strung on the hook so that a two to three inch trail hangs enticingly from the shank will score most often. Think about it from the fish's point of view: How often do you think they come across a huge pile of shucked clams all strung together? It certainly isn't a daily occurrence in my neck of the woods. A single clam waving gently in the current has to look a little less suspicious than a big ball of skimmers hung limply near the bottom. For anglers fishing where haddock are a possibility, using small baits is also necessary because this species has a mouth that is considerably smaller than that of a cod.

**Heavy tackle is usually required for cod as these fish
can weigh over 60 lbs. Here a double header taken on a
jig and teaser puts an angler's tackle to the test.**

As codfish are a highly suspicious breed, baited lines must be kept
stationary at all times to prevent spooking the fish. As with blackfishing, the sinker should be left to sit on the bottom with no jigging motion, save to check baits from time to time. If there is a roll to the sea,
lift your rod tip up and down with the heave to add or subtract line from
the water and keep your bait from jumping. Of course, even though the
bait is best left still on the bottom, it is important to keep a tight line so
that bites can be detected.

Some private boaters will chum for cod, cracking skimmer clams and
tossing them over the rail. You have to be careful when doing this in
deep water, however, as strong currents may deposit even a heavy clam
a considerable distance from your stern -- possibly drawing the fish away
from your baits. Chumming over codfish cover also frequently draws
bergalls and other pests. If the cod are biting better than a slow pick,
its probably best to forget the chum and leave well enough alone.

The Ultimate Party Boat Trip:
Overnight to the Grand Banks or Offshore Wrecks

Over the past ten years or so, overnight trips to far offshore locations have become increasingly popular among the party boat crowd, especially at New England and New York ports. For the most part, these ventures center around codfishing but quite a few other gamesters such as halibut, tilefish, hake, wolfish, and anglerfish can get into the act.

Ranging in length from overnight to four or five days at sea, these trips can cost anywhere between $75-$350. Most anglers, however, quickly agree that the price is well worth the investment as catches in terms of quantity and quality are usually outstanding. In fact, eight hours fishing at the Grand Banks frequently results in catches of over 250 lbs. per person (a rather conservative estimate) with the pool winning fish often weighing in the high 40's to mid 50's.

Sturdy equipment is needed for this fabled fishing. Nothing less than a 4/0 reel and stiff rod will do. Setups must be able to tolerate fishing with one pound of lead or 18-24 ounces of jig, and some days even more weight is needed. Forty pound test line is standard.

Only the larger boats sail on these trips. Most of these are well prepared for overnight fishing with sleeping bunks below deck. Since the number of bunks is limited, however, reservations are virtually always required.

Fishing here differs little from any other cod fishing except that the water is often considerably deeper, the tides stronger, and the fish bigger. Pool winners often exceed fifty pounds and frequently it takes a sixty pound fish to walk away a winner. There have even been a few cod taken from these waters exceeding the seventy pound mark! One other difference is the amount and size of incidentals taken. A thirty to forty pound wolfish is always a possibility and halibut weighing two hundred pounds or more have been taken. Huge hake and pollock can also mix in. On the standard cod grounds closer to home these fish are encountered but are usually smaller and less numerous.

If you intend to head out on one of these trips, bring along plenty of dry clothes as getting wet the first night can make things a little soggy for the next day or two if you do not have *at least one complete change.*

This 48 pound wolf fish (top) hangs in the galley of the Viking Star of Montauk, N.Y. It was taken on an overnight trip to the Grand Banks. Halibut (right) is one of the many surprises awaiting anglers on Grand Banks trips.

Cod usually strike with a decided "Thump! Thump!" although during the dead of winter they may bite more gingerly. A slight pause (a count of two or three seconds depending on the day) is often necessary before setting the hook. Although cod have big mouths, they do seem to need a second to get the entire bait down their throats. When you think the time is right, really put some muscle into setting the hook because you'll have to account for line stretch even before driving the hook into the hard mouth of your deep water prey.

Over the past ten years or so, jigging for cod has been steadily gaining acceptance to the point where it is now used more than baitfishing in some ports. It has been popular for years from Maine to Massachusetts, where huge schools of sand eels and herring can be counted on as the mainstay of the cod's diet. In the last decade, however, these baitfish have established themselves in more southerly waters, helping to make jigging productive as far south as New Jersey. Jigging is usually done on the drift although it can also produce at anchor. Due to the depths you must probe heavy jigs are the rule with 8, 12, 16 and 24 ounce weights most popular. This fishing differs greatly from bluefish jigging. For the most part the jigs are worked within ten feet of the bottom at all times. They are also worked more slowly. To jig a cod, simply lower your lure all the way to the bottom and then retrieve 10 to 15 cranks of the reel handle at a smooth, slow and steady pace. After the cranks are completed, disengage the reel and allow the jig to flutter back to the bottom. Set the hook hard as soon as you feel the slightest bump.

Large diamond jigs (top) are often needed to hold bottom at the Grand Banks and other offshore locations. Double-header pests (bottom), dogfish and bergalls, are a common nuisance when codfishing.

When party boating over open bottom, some of the more seasoned codfathers cast their jigs as far as possible in the direction the boat is drifting. This allows them first crack at the fish. Of course, this casting is accomplished with an underhand heave. The bow of the boat, specifically the pulpit, is the most favored position when attempting such casts as the lure can be swung under the boat and then heaved forward to gain the most distance. In general, winter and early spring codfishing is done over open bottom; early spring, summer and fall action usually takes place over wrecks or structure. Obviously, jigging is a less expensive proposition when the fish move away from potential snags.

While cod have often been compared to an old boot when questions of heart arise, I feel that they give quite a respectable account of themselves. This is especially true of any fish over 15 lbs. These fish make you work very hard to break them from the bottom and a lunker may make some exciting, dogged runs. After hearing so much about how poor a fight cod put up, you'll be quite surprised to hear how many anglers tell tales of the big one that got away. The problem with cod, in terms of their fight, is that after they have been reeled 80 feet or so from the bottom they come down with a case of the bends and thus lose a lot of desire. Up until that point they can put up one heck of a bullish battle.

One of the most exciting aspects of codfishing is the fact that you can never be sure just what you've hooked into until it comes to the surface. Some codfishing by-products are highly prized while others are less desirable. Among those fish bringing grunts and groans of frustration are the ever present bergalls and that spring and late fall pest, the spiny dogfish. A common summer visitor to the stern of codfish boats is the blue shark, which seems to fear nothing in this world and if presented with the opportunity will take a healthy chop out of a cod being reeled up. As an example, I once saw a man lose a $300-plus party boat pool when a large blue shark bit what might have been a 30 lb. cod in two about twenty feet below the surface. As it had been a slow day, the head and gills that the unlucky angler managed to retrieve still just missed taking second money in the cod pool!

Among the welcome incidentals most commonly taken are conger eels (a ling-like creature weighing one to five pounds); bulldog blackfish to 15 lbs.; humpbacked porgies and seabass; monster bluefish; the hard fighting and delicious pollack or "Boston Blue" which runs 5 to 30 pounds and fights like a giant bluefish; white hake which have a belly like a keg and can exceed 70 pounds; haddock, generally between three and ten pounds and highly prized as table fare; wolfish to 50 pounds; anglerfish (monkfish) which may exceed 75 pounds; and finally, giant Atlantic Halibut which usually weigh between 20 to 50 pounds but can exceed 250 pounds on occasion. With such possibilities, it's a wonder that the pay to play boats don't advertise "Codfish and Other Monsters of the Deep!" when hanging out their signs.

Chapter 16

⚓

Mackerel

Perhaps no fish common to east coast waters epitomizes the word action more than does the feisty mackerel. Each spring, great hordes of these miniature barracuda facsimilies invade coastal waters from the Carolinas to Maine, often chasing schools of sand eels or spearing ahead of them while simultaneously being pursued by an armada of fishermen and hungry blues. All this crowding and traveling must make the mackerel hungry, for he is an extremely greedy and aggressive character when it comes to supper time.

Because they lack a swim bladder, these pelagic fish are constantly on the move lest they sink to the bottom. Although relatively small compared to some of its better known relatives -- albacore, bonito, and some tunas belong to the same family -- mackerel possess the same qualities of speed and heart as these larger species, making them worthy adversaries of fishermen everywhere. Based on quality or quantity, the mack grades an "A" in my book.

By the second week of March, the macks have usually arrived off the Virginia coast in large numbers as the northward migration swings into full gear. At the height of the run, millions of them will file past the mid-Atlantic states on the way toward summering grounds in the Gulf of Maine and St. Lawrence Bay. It's been estimated that these fish travel northward at about six to eight miles a day. Thus, anglers in the more northerly states can roughly figure when the macks will arrive in their waters by keeping an eye on reports further to the south. Once the fish arrive, it's a good idea to get on 'em as quickly as possible because the period of red hot action is all too brief, often lasting only two weeks. In some seasons, the majority of macks migrate close to the coast, providing fantastic fishing close to port within easy reach of small boaters. In other years, the schools may choose to stay 15 to 20 miles or even further off the beach, making it quite a ride just to reach the fishing grounds. When that happens, party boating becomes the most logical option for getting in on the action. Mostly, prevailing winds and water temperatures dictate the course with cool water temperatures and winds from the north or east keeping the fish offshore.

As any mackerel fishermen will tell you, these small torpedoes probably respond better to artificials than any other fish in our waters, most days preferring lures to real bait. This is great for fishermen looking to fill their freezers as no time is lost to rebaiting hooks. It also pleases light tackle and fly fishing enthusiasts who are content to take their quarry one at a time and relish the chance to challenge predators with small jigs, spoons, plugs or silver streaked, streamer flies. With lures, silver or gold always seem to produce best. They can be presented on lines as light as four pound test (4X tippets) before breakoffs begin to be a nuisance. Of course with such light gear, multi-hook rigs must be avoided.

The choice rig among mackerel fishermen looking for quantity catches is a multi-hook setup known as a mackerel tree. Consisting of a series of small tube lures tied in-line above a four to eight ounce diamond jig or bank sinker, these can be homemade or purchased from virtually any coastal tackle shop for a price of two or three dollars. Mackerel trees are worked in two differing fashions: They can be jigged at a stationary depth with one to three foot lifts of the rod, or quickly retrieved with sporadic jerks thrown in to add spice. Both methods are usually performed from a drifting boat.

Since mackerel can be found at almost any depth from bottom to surface, the most important factor in provoking strikes is to locate the level at which they are feeding. Once this depth has been isolated, even the novice angler should experience fast action. Until the fish have been found, I recommend the quick retrieval method as it covers all possible depths. Once the first hits are felt, make a mental note of the depth and employ standard jigging. Some fishermen actually mark their lines with water resistant ink markers or electrical tape so that they do not lose the feeding zone of the fish, but I have never found this to be neces-

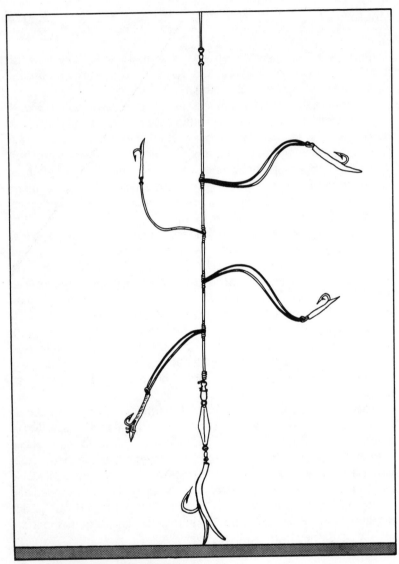

16a. MACKEREL TREE.

sary. I offer the idea though, in case you feel apprehensive about remembering the depth in the heat of action. Should you find yourself confused, simply ask a railmate or neighboring boater who is hooked up, "How deep?"

Although heavy spinning outfits can be used if the number of tubes is limited to two or three, sturdy boat rods and conventional reels are the choice of most fishermen when using mackerel trees. In fact, lines testing 15 to 30 pounds are the norm. At first glance this may appear a mismatch for the poor mackerel -- surely a two pound mack can't fight hard enough to warrant the use of 30 lb. gear. I agree 100% on that point, but when you consider the possibility of hooking three or four macks at the same time the need for heavy tackle becomes apparent. Four, two-pound mackerel hooked at once equate to eight pounds of fun -- all pulling in different directions and exerting great pressure on rod and reel.

Because mackerel aren't too big and can thus be easily controlled at the end of a rod, there are not as many tangles as one might expect when multi-hook rigs are the order of the day. Still, the largest fishing tangle I've ever seen occurred on a party boat mackerel trip. It wasn't the fault of any of the patrons, though. Instead, it was due to a private boater who trolled his wire- lined umbrella rig too close to our port side, snagging over twenty rigs. In the ensuing tug-of-war, the combined strength of twenty-plus lines proved stronger than 30 lb. test wire. The umbrella rig, by the way, was hung from the top rail of the upper deck in case the private boater proved brave enough to ask for it back. He never did.

Once positioned in a location known to harbor a good supply of macks, experienced skippers often resort to chumming with ground bunker. During the middle part of the season, when mackerel are most populous, chumming is not a necessity. As the schools begin to thin, constant chumming proves to be a great help in drawing and holding the fish.

In the eats department, when it comes to mackerel fresh is best. Macks do not have a generous freezer life and I find it best to make chum or chunk bait of those fish which will not be quickly consumed.

The only way I've eaten fresh mackerel is broiled, and I'd rate them only so-so. There are many people out there who do relish this oily fish, though, and I'm told that they are very good when smoked or barbecued. One thing is certain: whether or not I enjoy them as tablefare I do love to fish for mackerel, and each spring I suffer at least one "Big Mack Attack".

Chapter 17

⚓

Bluefish

The bright, hot sun beats down upon the heads of the party boat patrons. "Lower away boys", shouts the mate as the eager fishermen free spool their diamond jigs. "All the way to the bottom. Then crank like hell!" Within the span of three minutes, the entire starboard side is into fish! With rods arched toward the water, anglers jockey for position while passing rods over or under other fishermen, straining to gain the upper hand over the blue brute at the end of the line. Soon the call of "Gaff! Gaff!" is heard, and simultaneously the voice of disappointment in the background from an angler whose fish has broken off.

On another boat, another time, the moon is partially obscured by a cloudy sky as fishermen gently feed cut herring chunks into the night's darkness. Looking intent, they feel for a delicate tap signaling a pickup. The fishing begins as a slow pick, but builds in intensity as the chum slick calls in blues from the surrounding area. Within an hour, the fish seem to be racing each other for the baits, darting in and out of the boat's bright light like so many tiny blue and silver torpedoes. All one must do to hook up now is get the line in the water. Excited shouts of "Fish on!" punctuate the action. By the bewitching hour, the fishermen have already placed their rods in holders, aching arms finished for the night. On the deck, burlap sacks bulge, filled to the breaking point with the glistening blue of one of the ocean's most effective and aggressive feeding machines.

Ah, yes! Such is the demeanor of the bluefish that he is caught both day and night, on bait or lures, by novices and old salts. The favorite of many fishermen and staple of the charter fleet, more pounds of bluefish are taken per year by recreational anglers than any other east coast species.

Anglers love them for their fierce battles, and indeed, no fish shows more heart or greater determination to stay free. This noble champion

COURTESY THE JAMAICA, BRIELLE, NJ

Wherever and whenever they are caught, bluefish spell excitement! In recent years blues have been super plentiful, and private, charter, and party boats have all capitalized on it.

does not try so much to throw a hook as he does to confiscate it! Bluefish are also loved by party boat skippers and tackle dealers because they pack the boats with fishermen and wreck or steal enough tackle to generate a genuine cash flow. Rare indeed is the trip on which you will not lose at least one or two rigs to the razor sharp teeth or brute strength of this competitor.

Following on the heels of the mackerel schools -- one of their main prey throughout the early season -- bluefish arrive en masse between late May and July with southern ports getting first crack at the action. Working their way up the coast in a northerly direction, they will remain as long as the water temperature suits their metabolism and bait is plentiful. By late October, the blues begin to leave their northernmost haunts in favor of warmer southern waters and anglers switch over to other species in reverse order. With some northeast gamesters such as weakfish and striped bass currently weathering a period of (hopefully temporary) decline, it's highly probable that the bluefish will become even more important to the recreational fisherman and those who serve his needs over the next few years. Some caution must be exercised on this front too, though, since despite their apparent wide availability these days there is some question as to the vitality of worldwide stocks. Although it's difficult to believe based on catches over the past several years, many fisheries biologists now feel that the mighty blue is yet another popular species beginning a downward trend in population. In fact, one recent study suggests that the total biomass of these gamesters may now be but half of what it was in the early 1980's. With this thought in mind, you might strongly consider releasing some or most of your catch, even though it appears that for the time being there are plenty of fish to go around. Remember, it didn't take the striper very long to decline.

For the time being, bluefish are harvested in all sizes from ten inch snappers and two pound tailor or cocktail blues all the way to 15 to 20 lb. giant "gorilla gators". Depending on the time of year, port sailed from, and simply what's around, the tackle and methods used to capture these brutal savages will vary considerably. Like the striped bass, blues can be taken on live bait, chunk bait, plugs, surge tubes, umbrella rigs, poppers, bucktails and an assortment of tins and jigs. In fact during a bluefish blitz, you might be hard pressed to find an item these fish wouldn't strike. Nonetheless, there is usually a time and place where each technique does its best work.

One of the most consistent methods for taking bluefish of all sizes is

Bluefish fanciers would be well advised to carry a good assorment of jigs in different weights and sizes. For bait fishing, steel leaders reduce cut-offs and are used by most.

diamond jigging. Primarily a daytime procedure, and the most common modus operandi of party boaters sailing while the sun shines, this manner of fishing requires a great deal of work and exercise on the part of the angler. The object of the game is to make the lure imitate a sand eel, spearing, anchovy or other baitfish. For this kind of fishing, a sturdy six to six and a half foot conventional rod with plenty of backbone but a slightly sensitive tip is ideal. If possible, match this rod with a high speed 3/0 reel spooled with 20 to 30 lb. test mono. The jig is tied directly to the line via a clinch knot. Some anglers like to tie in a 50 to 80 lb. shock leader to help prevent cutoffs, but I find little need for this. Because of the tangles and excitement that accompany party boat bluefishing, anglers sailing on open boats may be better off with a slightly longer rod and 3/0 or 4/0 reel loaded with 30 to 40 lb. test mono (depending on the size fish expected).

Since no chum is used (most times) when jigging, skippers must get their boats directly in line with the moving schools of fish. Unless the choppers are really stacked up, this means a lot of short, action packed drifts. With the boat positioned ahead of the blues, the jig is flipped away from the direction of drift with an underhand cast (fishing from the pulpit affords greater casting distance to the party boater) or simply lowered over the rail. In either case, the lure is allowed to flutter unrestricted toward the bottom. Be sure to keep a thumb to your spool as bluefish are quite fond of striking jigs during their descent. The moment the jig strikes bottom, the reel is engaged and the fisherman cranks it toward the surface as fast as he can. Depending on the location worked and the mood of the fish, the jig may be reeled all the way to the surface or as little as five to ten turns of the handle before the process is repeated. The strike elicited from a hungry bluefish by a fast moving jig leaves little doubt in the mind of the angler that paydirt has been struck. Imagine yourself cranking the reel handle furiously when the jig suddenly stops dead in its tracks. You lean back hard trying to lift the rod, but it will not rise, only bend. Through the medium of line and pole, an angry pulsing is transmitted as the blue shakes its head from side to side in an attempt to rid itself of the metal parasite. Now realizing it has been hooked, it takes off on a powerful run and the battle begins.

The diamond jig owes its ability to closely approximate baitfish to its reflective qualities, shape, and size, plus unique action. Its silver sides are capable of reflecting light in water 150 feet or deeper. Shape, size, and the amount of light reflected can be chosen by the angler to "match the hatch". They may be worked fast or slow to entice various species of fish and can be worked from top to bottom. You can even cast them to breaking fish and whip them back just below the surface. Diamond jigs can have anywhere from two to eight light reflecting sides although the trend in recent years has been toward two and four sided jigs. Some are fat, some slender. Some are adorned with surgical tubes or bucktail, while others stand alone. One thing's for sure though: they all catch blues at times. Currently, there are a few companies experimenting with flourescent coated jigs to use at night and they seem to be enjoying at least some success. In spite of the popularity of jigs, though, bait still reigns supreme after dark.

Diamond jigs come in various sizes from two ounces on up to over 24 ozs. Party boaters will generally find weights of four to eight ounces the most useful while private boaters working shallow waters or inlet mouths with spinning gear as light as six pound test for cocktails may throw lures as small as an ounce. Note that hammered spoons such as the Kastmaster and Hopkins Shorty can be used in place of diamond jigs in shallow waters -- especially when small baitfish such as sandeels are in evidence. The idea is to use a jig which will closely approximate the size of the bait the blues are feeding on, while still cutting through rough currents or tides to get to the bottom as quickly as possible. The bottom is where these fish, like most inshore predators, spend most of their time.

On days when the jigs fail to produce, or after dark when there is not enough light to make most diamond jigs effective, many anglers resort to baitfishing. Intrinsic to this method of taking blues is establishing a chum slick. The chum -- traditionally a pungent, soupy mixture of ground bunker, herring, butterfish, mackerel or left over bait -- is doled over the side in foul smelling ladlesful. Drifting with the current, it seems to dissolve as it moves away from the boat, but enough usually remains in the stream to taunt the taste buds of any blue that crosses its path. Ideally, enough chum is ladled overboard to draw fish from the surrounding waters and to waiting baits without filling them to the point where they may choose to be finicky. While chum may be used from either a drifting or anchored craft, it is important that the slick formed remain unbroken so that the fish may find its source, and ultimately, your bait. For this reason, it's important to keep the chum flowing even when the fishing is hot.

Baitfishing can take many forms when the quarry is bluefish. For most, it can be broken into three main methods: freeline, bottom, and drail and chain. For all three methods, chunks of spot, herring, bunker, butterfish, mackerel or mullet (made by slicing these fish into two or three inch wide vertical segments) are the usual offerings.

Freeline is just what it sounds like, that is the fisherman allows his line to drift into the current unhindered. A thumb is kept to the disengaged conventional spool to control line flow and prevent runovers -- especially if a fish decides to hit hard. When a bite is detected, the reel is engaged and the rod is pointed toward the bait and then yanked upward at a right angle to the fish. Do not waste much time deciding when to set the hook for if too much thought is given to the matter the chances are that the fish will swallow your bait, hook and line deep enough to cut you off. Since a bluefish does have a tough mouth, it's also a good idea to set that hook more than once to ensure that the point of the matter stays in place.

The rigging used for this type of fishing, although modified to defeat the blue's sharp teeth, is uncomplicated. To prevent cutoffs, a 6/0 sproat or beak style hook preceded by a three to six inch length of wire leader is employed. This is simply tied to the main line or 30 to 40 lb. test leader via a clinch knot. If need be, a few split shots or a light trolling sinker can be added to take the bait down, especially when fishing in strong currents.

Bottom rigs are used when the blues are feeding deep, and they can be especially productive in harbor mouths or areas of strong current where drifted baits just won't stay in place long enough to give the fish a chance to find them. The standard bluefish bottom rig is tied with the hook suspended from a dropper loop two to four feet above a 4 to 12 oz. bank or diamond sinker. As with freelining, it's wise to use a hook preceded by a short length of wire to prevent cutoffs.

The drail and chain approach entails the use of a unique setup to keep the bait near the bottom and defeat the teeth of large blues. From what I've read, it was first developed on Long Island's famed Cartwright Grounds and thus, is often call the Cartwright rig. This procedure utilizes a drail of 6 to 12 oz. rigged with a swivel. To this is attached a heavy-duty split ring and a four to eight inch length of chain (no kid-

Big Blues Are Great Fighters

ding! In fact, window sash is the most frequent choice). An open eye 8/0 or 10/0 O'Shaughnessy style hook is attached to the swivel and a second hook to the chain's end. Whole or chunked baitfish, usually herring, bunker or butterfish, are then impaled once through the eyes or mouth with the forward hook and through the back, tail, or stomach with the trailer. This rig allows the bait to hang suspended at the chosen depth without allowing the it to bunch up or fall from the hook upon retrieve.

There are of course several variations to this rig. For example, on those nights when the fish are intent on committing suicide you can

DICK MERMON

Live lining big baits, like this bunker impaled on a treble hook, is a surefire way to incite the fury of marauding monster blues. It may also result in a more subtle pickup from a trophy sized striped bass, weakfish or doormat fluke.

substitute a large snap for the lead hook. This will make hook removal faster and safer as there will be but one point to tend. The Cartwright setup is normally employed in offshore areas where strong tides and big fish are the rule (such as off Nantucket, Cashes Ledge, the Cartwright Grounds, and in Block Island Sound), for the teeth of a 12 to 20 lb. blue can make short work of lines and leaders -- even if they test at 100 lbs.

Outfits for baitfishing should be quite stout. Remember, you are handling a lot of lead, heavy baits, unusually strong currents, and very powerful fish. When party boating for big, offshore blues, I like to bring along my favorite cod stick, one that is matched with a dependable 4/0 reel that features a "power handle." This rod is just shy of eight and a half feet. It has plenty of backbone and allows me to really apply pressure or lead my fish in a desired direction when it gets close to the boat. Although I prefer this particular setup, any stout stick of six feet or so, matched with a quality conventional reel packed with 30 to 40 lb. test mono, should be able to get the job done. Private boaters can get away with much lighter tackle, say a 3/0 conventional style reel, stout five and a half to six and a half foot rod and 20 to 30 lb. test lines. In some instances of shallow water action, medium to heavy spinning gear can get the job done and add thrills to each battle.

During the heat of summer, inshore bluefishing can get a little picky. While the party boats may be taking plenty of fish several miles off the beach, private boaters often go begging during July and August. At these times, a trolled umbrella rig will frequently take fish early in the morning or late in the day. Medium to large blues can sometimes be intercepted by trolling across the ocean end of inlets or up and down the beach adjacent to inlet, harbor or rivermouths. If nothing else, these same areas should produce reliable catches of cocktail blues. Trolling can be accomplished with wire line if the fish are deep but I've done just fine with 200 feet of 30 lb. test mono when looking for blues. Three to four inch green or white tubes seem to be the best producers whenever fishing is done close to the beach.

A couple of words of caution are in order before you head out to do battle. First off, you'll notice I've spoken quite a bit about those ferocious teeth. Believe me, this is one solid set of dentures. Take care when unhooking a chopper as they are quite capable of severing a finger if given half a chance. *Children should never be allowed to unhook bluefish!* Second, do not try to lift any large fish over the rail without the aid of a gaff. This is especially so on party boats where anglers often have five to twelve feet between them and the water. A jig or drail tearing free from a fish's mouth as you attempt to swing it aboard can become a very dangerous projectile. Impaling it in somebody's head is no way to make that person's day.

Bluefish are fabulous fighters and teamwork between passengers and the crew is vital to keeping lines from tangling and fish from being lost. Bringing a big blue to gaff takes a few minutes. Play the fish out rather than cranking it right in. "Green" fish close to the boat can really create some nasty problems. If you hook into a big blue and it begins to run, follow it around the boat. To avoid tangles, step under or pass your line over the rods of your fishing partners as you work your way to the bow or stern. Give each other plenty of room and lots of courtesy and everyone should catch some fish and have a good time.

One of the nicest aspects of bluefishing, aside from the fact that it occurs during the warmer part of the year, is that, at times, some real surprises mix into these catches. I've taken or witnessed the taking of weakfish, striped bass, bonito, false albacore, and both yellowfin and bluefin tuna while bluefishing and I can tell you that the anticipation and excitement generated by these incidentals have etched some exciting memories in my mind.

Although they can be taken throughout the summer months, the best time to head out for blues is during the fall run when they begin to head south in large schools. At this time of year, the blues can be counted on to show almost daily at many inlet, harbor and rivermouths. They may even be taken by working big blue, white or yellow poppers on top at this time of year, offering anglers enough thrills to last the upcoming winter as the choppers race each other to explode on lures splashed across the surface. No matter the method, as a rule, the later into September, October, and November you go, the larger the fish you're likely to encounter. Blues have been caught on Christmas Day from boats as far north as Block Island Sound, but most anglers close out on these gamesters by late November.

Part IV:
Odds
And Ends

L.T.M.A.L. - "Little Things Mean A Lot."

It's a phrase from a 1950's song by Kitty Kallen, and my parents frequently used this abbreviation at the end of written messages between themselves. The intent, of course, was to remind each other that all the little thoughts and actions each day added up to a successful marriage. It worked for over 29 years!

I was about 16 years of age when I finally broke their code, but it would take another four or five years before I would realize that this phrase could also apply to fishing. You see, all the little thoughts both positive and negative, and all those seemingly insignificant decisions and actions made during the course of each trip, play a vital role in determining your eventual fishing success. Pay attention to the small details, and the larger picture should take care of itself.

Planning a charter or rental trip, keeping a log book, choosing the right hook and tying strong knots, caring for the catch, cooking your rewards -- it all adds up to the complete fishing experience.

And, it can all be summed up in a single phrase: "Little Things Mean A Lot."

Chapter 18

⚓

Some Thoughts On Charters And Rentals

Amidst an armada of six to ten pound bluefish swirling on the surface not half a cast from the stern, my wife Tina hauled aboard a nine pounder that had belted a diamond jig. It was a late July evening and all was right with the Long Island Sound bluefishing off Centre Island Reef, just a short run to the west of Northport Harbor. Skipper John Alberta of Sound Charters twisted the jig from the fish's vice-like jaws and tossed the blue unceremoniously into the cooler.

"Typical fish for this area at this time of the year", he commented, while wiping his hands clean. "We've had them here almost every morning for two weeks. Evenings have been a little spotty, but it looks like they're setting up pretty good now. We should have fish here right into September."

To my right, a big blue shot out of the water and came crashing back down with a thud that sent a sparkling spray of sunlit droplets three feet into the air and left a huge whirlpool where the fish re-entered. A second and then a third fish, erupted from what appeared to be the same portal.

"They're probably feeding on rainfish (anchovies) -- a small minnow" announced our skipper. And indeed, the boat's chart recorder was marking plenty of both blues and bait.

On the surface, the choppers continued to roll, leaving huge boils and floating, sometimes frothy, bubbles wherever they surfaced. For forty minutes we hauled fish after fish, but as I glanced around at the two-dozen or so other boats working the schools, I noticed only three others that were hooking up with any consistency. It was then that I began to appreciate the benefits of having a knowledgeable captain at the helm. While the other boats, mostly small private craft, trolled or drifted across the reef, our skipper was keeping us virtually in place by stemming the tide. The technique, which he explained to us before we ever removed our rods from their holders, required that we lower our jigs to the bottom, crank up seven to ten turns, and then free-spool back to the bottom again. Most of the hits would come on the dropback or first two cranks. It was Alberta's job to keep the boat in place as we teased the fish.

Despite the numbers of blues apparent on the surface, our captain assured us there were even more near the bottom. The choppers, however, had been a little finicky for the last two days and seemed to have an infatuation for only those jigs which danced deep while moving neither far forward nor dropping back with the tide. Both Tina and I had connected within five minutes of flipping our lines over the side. For that we were glad, for we had passed up a day with the rental skiff fleet at Mattituck, 30 miles to the east, where rumor had it that scup were plentiful and big. As long as the bluefish action was hot, the porgies could wait for another day.

The sun was beginning to sizzle on the water now as it slowly sank below the horizon. Tina dropped her jig back to the bottom again, knowing the time to leave was almost at hand. In less than a minute, she was into another bruiser. "That puts me four up on you, Mr. Fisherman", she quipped as the blue hit the deck. It was obvious that she had mastered what for both of us was a new technique. Prehaps she had listened more intently while our mentor offered his instructions. I shrugged as the skipper gave a smile. "Ladies' Day, I guess.", was all I could muster.

Charter and rental boats: two other options for getting to the fishing grounds, each with their own dedicated followings. Each offer a world of piscatorial opportunities. Each, with a little planning and homework, can prove as productive as the best day on any private boat. We've talked at length about party boating as an option for those who don't have their own means of getting out. But it must be acknowledged that not everyone is endeared to or cut out for that kind of fishing and, even if they were a party boat port will not always be at hand. Even for those who find contentment on the head boats or who have access to private craft, a trip aboard a charter or rental boat may be just the right prescription from time to time -- especially when sailing on new waters or for unfamiliar species.

CHARTER BOATS

Charter boat fishing offers its patrons several advantages over other means of fishing. You could say that it sort of combines private boat fishing with party boating. The same Capt. Alberta mentioned above believes that charters are ideally suited for those people who fish only occasionally. To him, one of the major advantages patrons are paying for is the skipper's knowledge. This is similar to party boat fishing in that it's the captain's responsibility to find the fish and figure out how best to catch them. Since he's on the water four to seven days a week throughout the season (or even the year) the chances are usually pretty good that he'll have an idea about where to find the best action. As illustrated above, he may also have some tricks up his sleeve that even finicky fish can't resist. But, Alberta points out, there are other advantages, too.

First, those who sail on charter boats get to choose their railmates. Charters almost always consist of a small group of friends who are likely to have a good time even if the fish aren't biting. With most charters licensed to carry only one to six passengers, there isn't any crowding and the fishing tends to be a little more relaxed, with less frustration, more cooperation and fewer tangles than sometimes occurs on party boats.

Anglers can also use their own tackle or that supplied by the boat, and rarely are there additional fees for tackle use, lost jigs, bait or chum. Better still, special trips can be worked out to fish with a particular kind of tackle, say ultra-light, fly, or spinning gear, as opposed to the meat fishing tackle required to do the job right from a head boat. In general, charter boats tend to keep their rental gear in very good condition.

On a "good boat", one of the most enjoyable aspects of charter boat fishing is close interaction with the skipper. Throughout the trip, he'll be right at your side, ready with a little advice or insight when it's needed. When he speaks, it's time to listen -- for how often do you get a whole day to chat in depth with a person who catches fish for a living. What

A Few Ideas on Preventing Seasickness

No matter how strong your sea legs, there sooner or later comes a time when the water is stronger and your knees feel as limp as a cheap mono leader. Until only recently, there wasn't much one could do to prevent motion sickness, but advances in the medical field have led to vast improvements in this area. Chief among these is the drug Scopolamine. Available by prescription in the form of dermal patches, it is inexpensive at roughly $2.50 a shot and seems to prevent wooziness and nausea in many who find this disorientation an all too common affair. These patches are simply stuck behind the ear (à la band aids) where they allow their medicine to slowly seep through the skin and into the bloodstream. This medication has become so popular among the offshore (especially codfishing) crowd that it no longer even rates a double take. In fact, mates on some charters and party boats use it daily! So far, the only side effect of note is a drying out of the mouth. Bringing along a Thermos or canned beverage can resolve this problem. If you do obtain this or any other seasickness medicine, read directions. You may need to administer it several hours before the boat leaves port, as most of these take a little while to work their magic.

For those who are caught without any medication—a frequent occurrence when the morning looks calm but the afternoon roughs up—there are a few steps that may help to ease discomfort. First of all, stay away from the bait or chum buckets and the stern of the boat where the lingering smell of diesel smoke or gasoline can be the last straw for a person who is barely maintaining grace. Better to head up to the bow where the air is fresh and free of fish odor. Second, stay away from any food but dry crackers. Finally, focus your vision on the horizon, especially if land is visible, rather than at the wash in the boat's wake. This will help provide a focal point for your body to orient itself with.

Outside of these tips, there isn't much one can do about getting seasick. Just try to ride it out as gracefully as you can, and don't worry about what "the guys" think. Sooner or later we all get had!

an opportunity to learn first-hand the secrets of your favorite species or waters. Sometimes it takes a few trips to find a boat and captain you'll feel comfortable with, but once you hit it off right, you'll have a familiar face to look forward to each fishing season.

Charter boats today fish both inshore and off, but there are some differences between the two that one should be aware of. Let's start

with price. Inshore bay, sound or ocean fishing usually runs between $200 and $350 for a full day on the water. These trips are made for all the species discussed in Part Three. Offshore charters, usually for tuna, shark or billfish, can run from $350 to $800 with some trips lasting overnight. A tip for the mate should be included in your budget. For all charter trips, reservations are needed and at peak season in some ports you may have to book four or five months ahead of time to get the best dates. Generally, it's up to the patrons to decide which species will be the day's (or night's) target. This is usually taken care of while making reservations. Trips may be custom designed to meet the wishes of those who will sail. Perhaps it's a 50 lb. red drum or striped bass that holds your group's fancy, or maybe the day's intent should be to fill the freezer with cod, sea trout or flattie fillets. For those who want the best of both worlds, it may be possible to troll or jig for trophies during the first half of the trip and finish up with some bottom bouncing. While the decision is usually made well ahead of time, there is always the chance that the boat can try a new approach if things aren't working out during the trip.

Over the last several years there has been some conflict arising between charter boat captains and their patrons over who keeps the fish. For the inshore boats the answer is cut and dry: the patron takes home the catch. On offshore trips, however, the skipper may stipulate that the fish belongs to the boat. This problem most often arises when tuna, swordfish or mako shark are the catch. All three species command a high price at fish markets and a substantial sum can be realized by the sale of fish in good condition. At $4.00 a pound for instance, a price not uncommon for bluefin tuna, a 400 lb. fish is worth $1600! Since the patron is unlikely to have the commercial license necessary to sell his catch, and probably doesn't have room in the freezer for four hundred pounds of fillet, the real argument here is who gets the money. To be fair, most boats now work out an agreement to reimburse the anglers part of their fee if the fish is sold at the dock. Even so, each boat has it's own percentages and ideas on the subject. For this reason, those who sail offshore are advised to make certain this topic is settled before reservations are confirmed.

Most of the rules of charter boat fishing fall along the same guidelines as established by the open boat fleet. There is more leeway, though. In certain situations, for instance, light tackle and overhead casting can be employed. Just use your common sense. Ask the captain if questions arise, follow standard safe boating procedures, and all should go smoothly. To increase the chances of having a fun outing, try not to put too much emphasis on the number of fish taken as an indication of success. That way, even if the fish don't cooperate you can still enjoy a pleasant day on the water. It's also nice if you can think of the captain and mate, if one is aboard, as part of your group. Include them in your conversations and pictures -- they like to have fun on the water just as much as you and your friends.

Finally, keep the consumption of alcoholic beverages within reasonable bounds, or better yet skip them completely. It's unfair to put your captain in the position of having to say "no more." When you are on his boat you are his responsibility and any of a variety of bad things can happen on the water to people who are tipsy. By the way, any form of illicit drugs will not be tolerated on today's charter craft. With the Coast Guard's "Zero Tolerance" policy in effect, a skipper could possibly have his boat confiscated by the government if a passenger is found to be in possession.

RENTAL BOATS

Taking a rental boat out from a fishing station really isn't much different than sailing on a private craft. Perhaps the most alluring aspect of this arrangement is the opportunity to be your own skipper without having to bear the weighty cost of owning your own boat. The setup is ideal for those who fish occasionally, those who just wouldn't get enough use out of their own boat. If you are knowledgeable in technique and local fishing hotspots, this may be your best choice. Even if you are not too familiar with the fishing grounds, you can always ask the person supplying the boat where to fish. After a few trips you'll begin to get a feel for the better spots. Many fishing stations provide a map of local hotspots and will tell you before you set out which locations have been producing best for the species you intend to pursue. If all else fails, follow the fleet -- some of the regulars must have an idea as to where the fish should be.

Since you are the skipper on your boat for the day, you can fish wherever you choose within the boundaries allowed by the fishing station. You can also sail at the time or on the tide you think is best, during the station's hours of operation (usually 6 A.M. to 4 P.M. or so). In short, the boat is yours for the day to do with as you see fit. If the fish refuse to bite, go ahead and take a break on the sands of the nearest beach, dig shellfish on a sandbar or shallow flat, or simply drift with the wind and tide. Whatever you want, within reason of course, is OK. You're the captain.

Although there are a few scattered places where ocean going vessels are rented, by and large rental fleets are located in relatively protected areas: a sound, bay, or large river for instance. Most boats will range from 14 to 16 feet with six to 15 horsepower motors. They usually seat three with tackle comfortably, though four can sometimes safely squeeze aboard. Rental prices generally range between $40 and $75 for the day. That's roughly $15 to $25 per head for a group of three. Add perhaps five dollars per person for bait, chum, hooks, lunch, etc., and you'll be all set to go. While the boats provided are far from powerhouses, they will get you safely to and from the fishing grounds as long as you drive responsibly. In terms of tackle needed, just bring whatever you would use if you were heading out on a private boat. For those who lack the proper gear, most fishing stations also sell and/or rent tackle.

Perhaps the biggest drawback to rental skiff fishing is what I call "the wetness factor". Most of these boats ride a bit low and it doesn't take high seas or gusty winds to put a little water at your feet. For this reason a good pair of boots are a necessity in cold weather. Waterproof foul weather gear that can be worn when moving between fishing holes, even in a moderate chop, is a good idea, too. It should be obvious that without a cabin, these craft also require one to dress warmly even in fair weather.

Since you are the captain for the day, you are responsible not only for the boat but for your passengers as well. Drive safely. Don't drink if you are doing the driving, and if you have never driven a boat before ask for some instruction at the dock before heading out. It takes only five minutes to learn the basics of small boat handling, and knowing that you have a good idea of what it takes to steer and control your craft will ease your mind as you pull away from the dock, allowing you to concentrate on more pressing concerns -- like setting the hook on that first fish of the morning.

Anglers renting small skiffs for the day often score big with bottom species such as flounder, porgies and fluke.

Chapter 19

⚓

Hooks And Knots: Making The Best Choice

Whether they fish from boat or shore, master anglers are extremely picky when it comes to hook selection. They understand that while there are now thousands of hook patterns in a wide range of sizes, each has been designed with a particular task in mind. To be sure, all hooks have similarities in that they must be able to quickly penetrate a fish's mouth and then hold tight without straightening out, bending or breaking. But shape, size, thickness, shank length, barb, and other features are determined largely by various characteristics of the specific species sought and by the baits and lures used for that species.

"I'm going bluefishing -- what kind of hooks do I need?" is a common tackle shop question. All too often, the response is along the lines of "Those ones on the wall marked bluefish." This is especially so when buying hooks in a large chain store instead of a tackle shop that specializes in fishing. The counter help almost inevitably points out standard, pre-packed hooks without checking to see if the size and style match the type of tackle to be used. If you really want to see your buckets begin to swell with fish, be fussy about your hooks. Note which brand, style and size hook works for you on those days when you are scoring well. Write it down in your log book so you won't forget. Then, the next time you grab some tackle before heading out you can ask for the hook you really want.

As mentioned, hook style is determined by several factors, the most obvious being the mouth qualities of your quarry. You wouldn't, for instance, use a codfish hook to catch flounder -- any neophyte angler can see that it would just be too large for the poor little flatfish to inhale. At the same time, the wide gap style hooks that I like to use for flounder would not be a good selection for blackfish. The problem here is more subtle; the barb on these hooks is a little too long to quickly penetrate the tough skinned mouth of a bulldog tog. If I were to be fishing in a location where both tog and flounder can be taken at the same drop, a fairly common occurrence in some locales, I would put aside my wide gaps and opt for something which could hook either fish with a fair degree of consistency. The standard Chestertown style flounder hook (#8 or #6) would be a good choice in this instance.

Decisions such as this can only become easy with increased familiarity of your own fishing grounds and situations, so don't fret over making the right choice all the time -- it will come as you begin to pay your dues. If you're not sure if species mix, check with your local tackle shop, a fishing friend or regular to the waters you intend to work. They can help you make the right choice.

A second consideration in hook design is the type of bait to be employed. Virginia style hooks, usually associated with blackfish, are made extremely strong and have a short point which not only makes it easy to latch onto the jaw of tog but also ensures that the hook does not get bent when inserted into the hard shell of a green crab. A light wire sproat style hook, useless for blackfishing, might be substituted for a larger style when small killies are used in place of strip baits for fluke. The fine wire will allow the killie to swim slightly off the bottom where it will be more visible to the flat predators than a bait anchored in the sand by a heavier hook.

The size and aggressiveness of your quarry also plays a part in hook design and selection. Strong, large and highly suspicious species such as striped bass require very strong hooks that are small enough to hide in a bunker chunk. At the other extreme, bluefish sometimes seem to prefer a bright gold or silver hook that flashes in the sunlight, and their large teeth certainly necessitate the use of long shanked or wire leadered hooks.

A common mistake of beginning anglers is to use hooks that are slightly too large for the fish sought. During the early part of the porgy run, for example, fishermen often show up with hooks designed to take two to three pound humpbacks while half to one and a half pound scup predominate in the catch. The result? A lot more cleaned hooks than porgies. When faced with the choice of hook sizes, opt for the smallest size practical because this will fit in the most mouths and increase your

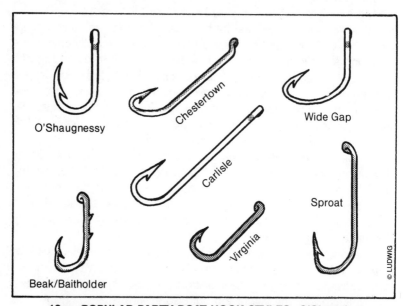

19a. POPULAR PARTY BOAT HOOK STYLES. O'Shaughnessy: Very strong and holds well. *The* **choice for tuna; Chestertown: A solid choice for flounder, the long shank makes for easy hook removal while the long barb ensures good holding ability; Wide Gap: Unique shape causes this hook to penetrate deeply, usually well up the shank. An excellent choice for flatfish or weaks; Carlisle: For many years the standard fluke and whiting/ling hook. Strong, long shank allows easy hook removal while thickness makes for easy handling; Beak/Baitholder: A quick penetrating hook, spurs on shank help keep the bait in place. A great choice for fast-biting species such as porgies; Virginia: Strong and extremely durable, this hook has a short barb for quick penetration of tough-mouthed species such as blackfish, cod and large sea bass. An excellent choice when working over wrecks and obstructed bottom or when using hard baits such as crab or conch; Sproat: The all around champion of hooks, this style can be used to catch virtually any species of fish anywhere in the world.**

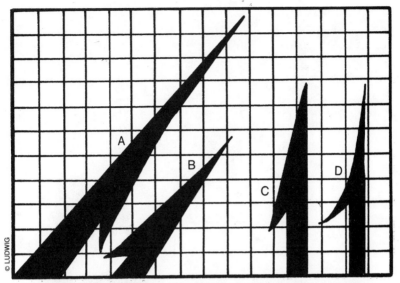

19b. HOOK POINTS. The shape and length of the hook point determines how well the hook penetrates and holds: a) Long points hold well; b) Short points penetrate quickly; c) Spear points are strong; d) Hollow points are finer and pierce flesh better.

catch throughout the day. You can't catch them if they can't take in your hook.

By the way, just because a hook has a point on it doesn't necessarily mean that it's sharp. Every hook you tie on your line should be sharpened before being used. Even new hooks right out of the bag need sharpening! Using an inexpensive (one to five dollar) file or sharpening stone, sharpen the tip of the hook on three sides, a process called triangulation. This creates three cutting edges that really dig into the fish's mouth. In fact, it can increase the penetration of a hook by as much as 4,000 times that of a brand new, never-been-wet unsharpened hook. I think you get the point about hook points: Don't be lazy. Sharpen each hook before using it and you will be duly rewarded. Hooks that have been used previously should also be examined for rust spots and bending. If you even slightly suspect something is wrong, discard it. It's not worth losing the fish of a lifetime over a 25-cent hook.

One last thought on hooks: Use bronze hooks instead of stainless steel whenever possible. Bronze hooks will rust out after a few days should a fish get away with a hook still embedded in its jaw. Stainless

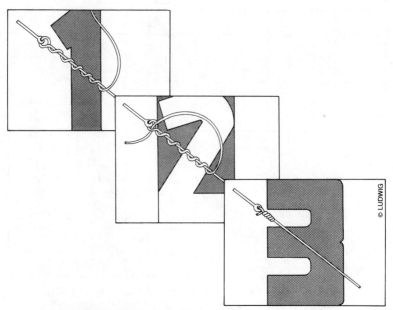

19c. CLINCH KNOT. Used for terminal tackle connections such as line to hook, line to lure, or line to barrel swivel. This is the preferred knot to use when working with lines of 20 lb. test or greater.

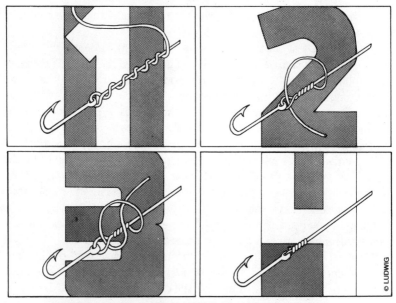

19d. IMPROVED CLINCH KNOT. Used for the same terminal connections as is the clinch knot, but with lines testing 20 lbs. or *less*.

steel takes a long time to corrode. With the bronze hooks, the fish has at least a chance to resume normal feeding habits after a few days, giving it a better chance to survive.

The accompanying drawing provides a look at some of the most frequently used hooks for east coast species. Take some time and examine the illustrations thoroughly so that you recognize each style by heart. That way, you will be able to easily identify what type and size hook your fishing partner is using if he's catching all the fish and you're losing all the baits.

Selecting the right style and size hook will help ensure that you connect with a few of our finned friends. Getting those fish into the boat, however, is another story. While many anglers fail at this task because of poorly set drags or a lack of knowledge in terms of fighting a trophy fish, the place where most go astray is in the knots department.

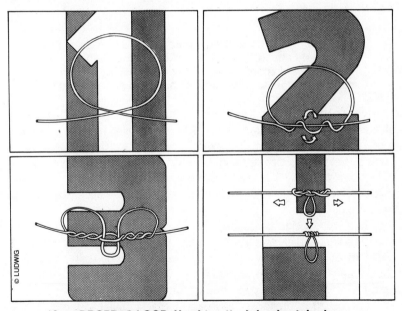

© LUDWIG

19e. DROPPER LOOP. Used to attach hooks, tube lures, teasers or sinkers to an otherwise unknotted section of line. This knot forms a versatile loop. The position of this loop also determines the distance between hook and sinker. To attach a teaser, tube or snelled hook to a dropper loop, pass the loop through the hook eye or leader knot and loop the lure or hook completely through the dropper loop. Tighten by pulling leader or hook and dropper loop in opposite directions.

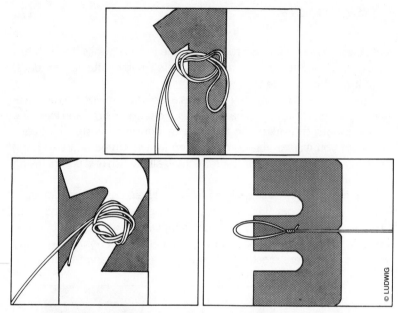

© LUDWIG

19f. END LOOP. Used to tie a loop in the end of a line for quickly attaching leaders, sinkers, etc. Attach tackle in the same manner as with dropper loops. Be sure to make this loop large enough for sinker to pass through.

It's not necessary to learn any complicated knots in order to succeed at the inshore game. In fact, if you know how to properly tie just the four illustrated in this chapter you should be in pretty good shape. Before you sit down to practice, though, be advised that knot tying is a subject to be taken seriously. Tying a knot improperly can rob your line of more than 50% of its rated strength, which may be just the break a big fish needs to get away.

There are few sights in fishing more sickening than a little curl at the end of the line which practically screams that the line broke because of a bad knot. The pain is so intense because it tells you that the big fish should never have gotten away; it was your fault and no one else's. Don't let this happen to you. Practice on shore before you go fishing. Practice, practice, practice! Become intimately familiar with each of the knots shown in the diagrams so that when the fish are biting, you will not need to take any unnecessary risks with knots that are inappropriate. Master these knots now and learn when to use each one. Then, when the fish of a lifetime comes along, you'll be sure he never gets to say "knots to you!"

Following are a few tips on knot tying:

1. Use plenty of line to allow you to complete tying your knot without difficulty.
2. Before drawing a knot up tight, wet the line with water or saliva for lubrication. This will prevent binding and allow the knot to tighten easily.
3. Draw each knot tight slowly. When two ends are involved, pull them slowly in opposite directions. Never tighten a knot with quick or jerky movements. These will cause heat to build, possibly weakening the line.
4. Allow at least one quarter of an inch of tag end on each knot. This will help prevent the knot from unravelling or slipping.
5. If your knot breaks repeatedly when tightened, check your hook or lure eye for rough spots that may be cutting it.

Chapter 20

⚓

The Value
Of A Logbook

Although many anglers dismiss it as a nuisance, keeping a fishing log book or journal can play a vitally important role in your success.

Keeping a log book should be neither time consuming nor involved -- ten minutes tops! The information you compile in this short amount of time can make a big difference in your consistency. Of course, there will be times when you completely disregard every entry you've ever made, play a hunch and come out smelling like a rose -- or better yet, a mackerel. But this is much more the exception than the rule. Within this chapter is a reproduction from my log book detailing one of my favorite fishing trips. You can set up your own log book in similar fashion or make any changes you feel are necessary. Just be sure to include each of the variables discussed below in one form or another and you will get the most important information in print.

DATE

This is pretty self explanatory but a must for any fishing log. You'll find that after several years of record keeping, you can check your entries from previous seasons and find that the fish arrive at each different fishing hole at a set time each year. While the date is rarely exact, it is usually within a week or so. Recording the date of each trip will help take the guesswork out of choosing a place to fish. You may note, for instance, that fall blackfish action in your area usually begins about the second week of September on inlet jetties or over shallow inshore ocean wrecks. A look through entries of the past two or three seasons may further reveal that these fish move to mussel beds or rocky areas inside a bay or harbor two or three weeks after the first fish are reported at the jetties. No bays or harbors in your area? Perhaps they move east or west or from 60 foot depths to 30 feet of water or in some similar manner. Your records may show that the season always peaks within two or three weeks of this move. You now have a rough schedule to follow and much of the guesswork as to when a trip should be planned is taken away. Cross reference your most productive dates with other categories such as location, tidal stage, weather and sea conditions and it should be relatively easy to pick a productive spot at which to begin your fishing day. Recording the date of each trip will help you chart the productivity of various fishing holes throughout the season. It should also help prevent you from missing out on the peak of activity for those species you most like to pursue.

LOCATION FISHED
Under this heading, list each and every place where you wet a line during your trip. Even if you didn't catch any fish at a particular spot, jot it down. You'll soon see patterns develop indicating which locations produce best at different times of the day or season, with winds from a certain direction, or on one tidal stage or another. Throughout the log, break all your information down by location whenever possible (i.e., list species caught at each location, note tidal stage at each location, etc.).

WEATHER CONDITIONS
Let me start by saying that it has been my experience, and my log backs me up on this one, that most popular east coast species bite better under cloudy skies. Whether this is a result of pressure changes from moving weather fronts or reduced sunlight I can't determine, but it may have a little to do with both. Weather conditions generally play the leading role in determining if a trip is likely to produce acceptable results. Obviously, few anglers cancel trips because of sunny skies but it should also be noted that light rain or moderate cold do not always mandate trip cancellation. These two factors can be dealt with through proper clothing and rain gear. Of course if it's going to pour, there is no reason to head out and be miserable, but fishing in 30 degree temperatures in late

Camera Tips

Bringing along a camera is a sure fire way to record the enjoyment and thrill associated with a successful fishing trip. Clear, high quality pictures make reliving the experience and showing off to friends that much better.

Remember that salt water is corrosive, so keep your camera in a waterproof bag or carrier when not in use and wipe it down with a moist rag at the end of the day. Also, always wear the safety strap around your neck. Footing is never a sure bet on the water and losing your balance and dropping a camera overboard will not make for many smiles.

With the automatic cameras on the market today, taking a nice, clear photo isn't as difficult as it once was. You'll find that 200 speed film shoots very well during daylight hours but for early morning or late evening shots, 400 speed is better. Don't be afraid to use a flash if the sky is overcast or you are shooting on the side of the boat away from the sun.

A common pitfall that should be avoided is taking pictures while facing into the sun. This will result in shadowed faces and silhouettes. Always try to position yourself and your subjects so that the sun is at your back and in their faces. Remove hats whenever possible to prevent facial shading. You can partially compensate for these backlit situations by using your flash. This is called "fill-in" flash.

Finally, try to take action shots whenever possible. The classic dead fish photo is great when someone is holding up a monster fish, but photos of yourself or friends unhooking or fighting fish are usually much more interesting when viewed by others. Storing your photos (in an album or whatever) in a beginning-to-end format is also a way of adding life and meaning to them.

December or through a light summer rain is not all that uncomfortable when the fish are biting. More important than sunshine or clouds are wind speed and direction and their effects on local wave heights, tides, water clarity, and fish migrations.

For any type of east coast fishing that takes place more than a mile or two offshore, strong winds (18 knots or more) from the northeast, east or south are likely to kick up seas which will make bottom fishing difficult at best. Cod, sea bass, and blackfish trips are especially vulnerable to choppy seas, as it is difficult to keep a line stationary on the bottom and hard for skippers to anchor up over select wrecks or bottom structures. Additionally, it becomes increasingly tough to net or gaff large fish when the boat is bouncing up and down. This is especially true for the bow gang on a party boat which may have it's deck ten feet above the water to begin with. In some locations, strong winds from a particular direction may make fishing more difficult on a specific tidal stage. A look through my log book shows that blackfishing off the Con-

---

DATE: May 26-27, 1980   **RATING:** 10+

BOAT AND LOCATION: Viking Star, Montauk NY
Overnight "Nantucket Wreck Trip"

WIND DIRECTION: SW 5-12 knots   **AIR TEMP:** 50-65°

SKY: Sunny   **TIDE:** Slack → high

WATER CONDITIONS: Very Clear   **MOON:** 1/2

WAVE HEIGHTS: 1-3 feet   **COST:** $75.00

NOTES: Fished with Dad over several wrecks including the "Andrea Doria". Had a great day - Dad won the cod pool for $160.00! The fish weighed a little over 65 lbs. and a fell for 6 glob of clam. Worked spots 9-10 (bow to midship) and between us caught 17 cod, 2 pollack and 2 hake. 4 cod were over 20 lbs., the rest 8-15 lbs. One hake weighed close to 35 lbs.

Used clam all day long until we switched wrecks and ended up with a lot of bergalls. Switched to conch to beat the bergalls and caught 2 cod over 20 lbs. Some guys on the bow used 16-oz jigs and did very well with pollack. Next time, bring some jigs to try for pollack when cod slow down.

20a. SAMPLE FROM AUTHOR'S LOG BOOK.

necticut coastline near Fisher's Island, for example, is often difficult when the wind blows hard from the north to northwest and the tide is retreating from Long Island Sound. Under these conditions, 12 to 20 ounces of lead are needed to hold bottom in 60 to 80 feet of water. Even with a moderate wind, the waves are so sharp here that keeping a bait stationary is next to impossible for most anglers. On the other hand, these same waters on the same tide with winds from the south or west require only 8 to 10 oz. of lead. Based on this information, I might decide to do my blackfishing in a more protected area such as Port Jefferson when the winds blow from the north. But if they are from the south, I'll definitely consider heading out to Fisher's Island for the large bulldogs that can be taken there under favorable conditions in the fall. It should be noted that strong north winds, while disrupting black-fishing at Fisher's Island, may be just what the captain ordered to get the fall migration of gorilla blues under way along the coast or to tighten up loose schools of sea bass in Delaware and Chesapeake Bays.

Too little wind can also be a problem, as many a becalmed bluefish jigger or fluke fisherman will confirm. For species taken on the drift, a slight wind when not working against the tide is actually preferable to flat seas. On those calm, mid- summer days when the water looks like a sheet of glass smeared with gently swirling fingerprints, it might be a better choice to do some porgy fishing or other bottom bouncing where you can easily anchor over a good piece of bottom and work bait without worrying if the tide will push hard enough for you to cover productive water at speeds which will make drifted baits or lures look enticing.

Prevailing winds sometimes play a part in changing water temperatures. In some locales, several days of warm southern winds may push enough warm water toward the beach to drive out species such as mackerel, at the same time bringing new, warm water arrivals. During the fall months, a few consecutive days of cold northeast winds send the blues, porgies, seabass and fluke into their fall migration patterns. All it takes is a change of a few degrees in water temperature and the fish respond one way or the other.

Finally, continuous strong winds can cloud up the water in some locations, giving it a murky appearance. My log has shown that, at times, this can adversely affect fishing probably because the quarry has difficulty seeing the bait. This is, of course, a location specific problem but it is quite common in shallow bays and estuaries.

TIDAL STAGE

Some species, such as weakfish, are very tide specific. They may feed on a single tide or single tidal stage for several weeks, eating little on other stages. While this tidal preference may change from week to week or year to year, certain locations seem to have a pronounced favorite. If you read in the paper that the fleet has been working a specific area, you can look in your log book and see which tide has the upper hand and plan your next trip to coincide with that stage of the tide. Fishing when the quarry should be in its best feeding mood will optimize your time on the water. This is easy enough for the private boater or someone taking out a rental skiff. They can simply head out a little before the optimal time and return when the bite has slowed. The party boater, however, must put a little extra thought into his or her planning. Let's say that the area you figure the party boat fleet will work has always produced best on incoming water during the spring weakfish run. You check the tide charts and find that incoming tide begins at 10:30 A.M. at that location. Knowing this, it might be a good idea to look for a boat that sails at 8:00 A.M., rather than taking your usual choice which departs at 6:00 A.M. The reason is, of course, that the later sailing boat will spend more time fishing on incoming water than will the early bird. Despite all the hype about fishing at dawn and dusk, in most inshore salt water fishing situations it is more important to fish the right tide than it is to fish early or late in the day.

Just as important as weather conditions in relation to tide is moon phase. In some areas, especially at inlets or on deepwater wrecks, banks and ledges, full and new moon phases cause the tides to become much stronger than usual. While this generally helps shallow water fishing, deep water anglers may be surprised to find that locations where four to six ounces of lead were enough to hold bottom suddenly require sinkers of 8 to 12 ounces. It might be wiser to fish such areas on 1/4, 1/2, or 3/4 moon phases.

SEA CONDITION

This is a little more involved than one might think at first, but keeping an accurate record of a few variables over the years should help reveal definite patterns. These patterns are what you should be looking for at all times. One never knows just where they'll show up, but frequently it's in this category.

Understanding the behavior patterns of the various species is a big key to success. You see, once you've become a master angler, further improvement of technique can only up your scores so much. Then, sailing under conditions which make it easier to fish or cause more fish to be around becomes the best way to increase productivity. When entering information on sea conditions, be sure to include wave heights, water clarity, and water temperature. It's important to note wave heights because for some species, once the waves reach a certain level productivity drops off sharply. Whether this is due to the difficulty holding bottom or presenting a lure properly, or because fish schools are scattered or broken by choppy seas (a common problem when mackerel fishing), knowing at what degree productivity drops off can save you wasted trips.

Water clarity should be recorded because in some locations and for some species, only a little murkiness or discoloration is enough to put the fish off their feed. In other spots and with other species, soiled water has little effect on the day's outcome.

Water temperature is the most important sea condition to note. After three or four years of note taking you can begin to establish temperature zones for each species. When working weakfish, for example, I don't bother sailing until the water's surface temperature is around 58 degrees. I'm not saying that you can't catch any weaks when above or below this, but by my experience it just won't be worthwhile. The beauty of record keeping is that, after a few years, you'll notice that the correct temperature is reached for each species at the same time each year, give or take a week or two. In the area where I do most of my weakfishing, for instance, the second or third week of May is when it usually all comes together. To get an accurate reading of water temperature, you'll need to purchase an inexpensive fishing thermometer. This can be tied to the end of your line and lowered to the level at which the fish are biting best to make a recording.

TARGET SPECIES AND INCIDENTAL CATCHES

Recording your target species and the number caught is pretty self explanatory. But also listing incidental catches allows one to know what other species to prepare for, and offers the chance to recall later what a ball you had on that trip when yellowfin tuna invaded a bluefish chumslick ("sure wish we had some tuna hooks on board because those brutes straightened out several bluefish hooks") or dense schools of three pound mackerel showed on the cod grounds ("next time remember to bring the mackerel trees!"). Be sure to list your catches by location should you fish in more than one spot on a trip.

BOAT NAME

While your friend will probably make it a point to never let you forget the fast action you both had when he skippered for the day, you may be surprised to learn that it really is hard to keep track of which boat caught what over the course of a few seasons of hard fishing. This is

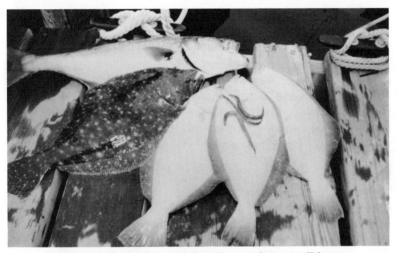

A well kept logbook can help tell you when conditions are right for catching species that sometimes mix. Fluke and school blues shown here often run together.

especially so for those who frequent party or charter boats. When sailing from a large port, or even a not so large one, it becomes easy to forget which boat produced best for each species. Every skipper has one kind of fish that he seems to catch just a little better than anyone else. You may also find a particular boat to have a pleasurable crew, great family facilities or adaptations for the handicapped. Having a great day and then forgetting which boat it was on can be really frustrating, so make it a point to always mark it down.

COST PER TRIP

The private boater, or those renting a boat for the day, will want to include under this heading gas, bait, chum, lunch, tackle, launching or rental fees, etc. Party or charter boaters should record the fare for the day plus tips, lunch, rigging and any pool money placed in the kitty. This will allow for easy comparison of prices between ports and fishing for different species. We all run a little low on dough at one time or another and showing up at the dock with just enough money to take a $25 trip when the fare is $27 can be as frustrating as it is annoying. Believe me, I know! (Party boats, by the way, do not accept credit cards or checks, except perhaps when you pre- register for special trips).

NOTES

This is an extremely important section for in it goes all that information for which there is no other provision on the page. Here it can be noted that there was an unusual amount of baitfish in the water, a different style hook produced superior results, you caught your biggest or most of a particular species, a good friend beat you out for the pool money, a new hole was found which you think could be worked from shore, or simply that you and a co-worker had a really enjoyable trip taunting your boss while the fish refused to bite.

RATING

This is not really necessary, but I rate each trip from one to ten based solely on the number and size of the fish taken. This allows me to flip through the log and quickly stop to note the conditions of any day with a high rating -- sort of a lazy man's index if you will. This way, I can find all the high ratings for a particular species and see what conditions each day had in common or compare low scores so I know when it's better to stay home and sleep.

Basically, that's all of a format you need to get started on your log book. Use the information you gather as a guide, though, not a bible. If all the conditions indicate poor fishing but it's your only day off, you'll probably go anyway. At least you'll know what to expect, and catching a few fish will make you feel that much better when you realize that you did it under less than perfect conditions. Best of all, on those cold winter nights when even the cod and whiting diehards say it's crazy to head out, you can sneak off into your, tell your wife that you are engaged in some very important fact compilation, and sit back and reminisce about the best trips you've ever taken.

Chapter 21

⚓

Proper Fish Care

"Wouldn't it be nice," my good friend Rick Lombardo once asked me, "if we could just go out and catch fillets?"

Of course, I don't know how much pleasure we would derive from their fight and I imagine a five pounder would no doubt be considered a nice catch by any standard. But I am certain that anyone who has ever punctured a finger while gutting a seabass or sliced a hand while filleting flatfish would fully appreciate the prospect.

This not being the case (and perhaps even if it were), fish which are not carefully chilled and handled are prone to bacterial invasion. This is especially true of those which are left to beat themselves on deck where they often puncture their skin before later being placed, very warm and quite dead, in a cooler or sack.

Of even more concern should be the fact that some bodily functions continue after expiration. Stomach enzymes, for example, continue to digest food long after a fish has died and if left uncooled, will begin to rot the fish's intestinal track. This process releases juices which quickly contaminate the flesh causing that sickening, "fishy" taste.

Proper fish care starts before the boater ever sails. What will you need to bring to ensure yourself and your family of a fresh, clean tasting dinner? You probably will need a cooler, you may very well need ice, and you may need packaging such as plastic bags, wax paper or freezer wrap; paper towels and rubber bands are other good things to have along.

Ideally, you should own a strong, sturdy, 64 to 151 quart cooler. These devices are capable of storing all the fish you're likely to catch on a single outing, plus the ice necessary to keep the fish cool. When choosing among coolers, look for those models which can stand up to the abuse and beating a flopping fish can dish out. Also, try to select a brand with a drain plug located at its base which will allow you to periodically release excess water and slime as the ice melts and fish pile up throughout the day. A cooler with a cushioned cover can also serve as an extra seat, especially in a small boat where such conveniences as sitting quarters are often at a minimum.

For those without coolers, a large clean trash can, buckets or burlap sacks will have to do. These items are obviously not quite as effective as are coolers but they have done the job for thousands of fishermen over the years. Burlap sacks should be soaked periodically during the course of the day. At no time should fish be left to sit in standing water no matter what storage device you employ. Also, stay away from plastic trash bags whenever possible. Many of today's leading brands contain deodorant scents which will be absorbed by any fish placed inside. Clear plastic bags are OK to transport fillets or cleaned fish for short distances when accompanied by ice, but left in the heat of a summer sun they tend to work like an oven, quickly reducing your catch to a pile of warm, mushy trash. No matter what you keep your fish in, keep them out of the sun as much as possible.

As far as ice is concerned, over the course of a full day block ice holds up the best. It can be purchased at a local store on your way to the dock or you can make it at home by filling a few empty one gallon milk containers with water and placing them overnight in your freezer. I like to use the milk containers because the ice stays separate from the fish. Placing your catch directly on ice may cause discoloration -- harmless but not exactly appetizing.

The major advantage of block style ice is that it does not melt as rapidly as do cubes or crushed ice, and so it allows your catch to stay cooler for a longer period of time. Remember, depending on your choice of quarry you may be spending a couple of hours to two days on the water. Placing five or six gallons of homemade ice or a block or two of the store bought variety in your cooler should last almost the length of a normal full day trip. It won't last nearly as well in a bucket or burlap sack, but it certainly will help. During the winter, of course, ice is not as important but it's always a good idea to bring at least a little along. Better safe than spoiled.

Athough block ice is easier to deal with and holds up well over the long haul, some studies have demonstrated that burying your catch immediately in crushed ice or "slush" (made by mixing crushed ice or cubes with a small amount of salt water) is the fastest way to cool it down and prevent spoilage. If you are heading out on a short trip, say four hours or less, you might want to give this a try. Simply fill your cooler a third of the way with crushed ice or cubes and bury your catch in it so that each fish is completely covered. Don't forget to leave some ice under the fish. If your catch begins to exceed your ice supply, add a bucket of sea water to form "slush" and simply drop your fish in the mixture as each is caught.

If you find yourself in a spot with no ice available, you can minimize spoilage by immediately cleaning your fish. Remove the head and entrails to allow necessary bleeding and reduced enzyme contamination.

If you're on a party or charter boat, see if the mate will wholly or partially clean your fish on the way back to port. Give him a nice tip if he does. If you've been out on your own, clean the fish at dockside if you have the time and if there are facilities for this. You're going to have to do it later anyway, and it's better to leave the mess at dockside than to have to contend with it at home. Repack your cleaned fish in ice, preferably clean, unmelted ice, for the trip home. Keep cleaned fish, especially fillets, cold and dry them off with paper towels. Leave a roll of paper towels on the boat or in your car just for this purpose.

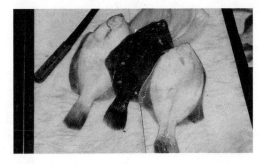

Chapter 22

⚓

Delicious Fish Recipes

Anglers list a wide variety of reasons why they go fishing: sport, relaxation, getting close to nature, having a good time, or just getting away from it all. In the back of almost everyone's mind, however, is the reward of fresh seafood dinners when they return home. I know that I can't wait to sink my teeth into a fat flounder fillet or a cod steak after a "hard" day on the water.

While most of us simply think of fish as delicious, the rewards of eating them go far beyond. Eating fish is healthy! They are easily digested, low in cholesterol, low in calories (if cooked without rich sauces), low in fat, low in sodium (that's right, salt water fish are actually lower in salt content than fresh water fish), and high in protein -- and they taste good! With this in mind I offer some of my favorite recipes in the following section and hope you will enjoy them.

Preparing fish takes little time in most cases. A simple rule to follow when cooking a fish you have never served before is to cook it 10 minutes for each inch of thickness, or until the meat just barely loses its translucence. For fillets or steaks, allow 1/3 lb. to 1/2 lb. of fish per person. Dressed or gutted fish require about 3/4 to 1 lb. per diner. Good eating.

FLATTIE ROLL-UPS
(Options: flounder, fluke, or other firm, white-fleshed fish)

12 large fillets
10 strips uncooked bacon,
  diced
1/2 cup melted butter
6 cups cornbread crumbs
  (from crumbled, pre-cooked
  cornbread)

1/2 tsp. dried chervil
1/2 tsp. dried tarragon
Hot water
Butter or margarine

Cook bacon until crisp; drain on absorbent paper. Strain bacon drippings; measure 1/4 cup and add to melted butter. Combine cornbread crumbs, bacon, herbs, and combined fats; mix well. Add enough hot water to make stuffing as moist as desired. Place a single spoonful of stuffing on each fillet; roll up firmly. Line baking pan with foil. Grease foil. Place roll-ups in pan and dot generously with margarine. Bake at 375 degrees for approximately 25 minutes, or until fish flakes easily with a fork. Serve with the sauce of your choice. Makes 6 to 8 servings.

BEER-BATTER-FRIED FLATFISH
(Options: flounder, fluke, whiting)

2 lbs. fillets cut into serving
  sized pieces.
1 1/2 cups flour
1 cup beer
1 1/2 tsp. salt

1 1/2 tsp. paprika
1 T. lemon juice
1 1/2 tsp. salt for sprinkling
  fish

Sprinkle fillets with lemon juice and 1 1/2 tsp. salt. Set aside. Pour beer into bowl. Sift together 1/2 cup of flour, salt and paprika into beer. Mix thoroughly with wisk until batter is light and frothy. Heat oil in deep fat fryer until it reaches 375 degrees. Roll and press fillets in remaining flour, dip into batter and fry in oil for about 3 1/2 minutes. Serves 4-6.

BROILED FLATTIES WITH FRESH VEGETABLES
(Options: flounder, fluke, striped bass or other white-fleshed fish)

1 lb. fillets
2 fresh carrots (med. size)
2 large stalks celery
1 small onion
1/2 cup lemon juice

1/2 cup butter or margarine
1/2 tsp. tarragon
1/2 tsp. paprika
Salt & pepper to taste

Arrange fillets in a glass baking dish. Season with salt and pepper. Thinly slice the carrots, celery, and onion and arrange over and around the fillets. Melt butter or margarine and pour over fillets and vegetables. Add lemon juice, tarragon, and paprika. Place in broiler for approximately 20 minutes. Serve with wild rice. Serves 4.

HAWAIIAN FRIED FISH
(Options: whiting, ling, flounder, fluke, sea bass, blackfish, porgy)

1 1/2 lbs. fish fillets, sliced into two-inch strips
1 cup flour, mixed with 1 tsp. salt and 1/4 tsp. pepper
Oil for deep-frying

Hawaiian Sauce:
6 oz. can pineapple chunks   2 T. cider vinegar
1/3 cup soy souce   1 T. grated onion
2 T. lemon juice

Combine all sauce ingredients in a small sauce pan. Cook over medium heat, stirring until very hot.

Pat fish strips dry with paper towel. Rub fish into flour mixture until well coated. Pour oil in wok to a three-inch center depth. Heat to 375 degrees. Fry fish strips in wok, four at a time, until lightly browned. Pour Hawaiian sauce over fish strips and serve while hot. A deep fryer or 10-inch skillet may be used in place of the wok.

TINA'S "FAMOUS" GOLDEN FISH NUGGETS WITH CHEESE SAUCE
(Options: blackfish, fluke, flounder, sea bass, porgy, whiting)

1 lb. fillets   1/2 cup mayonnaise
1 cup seasoned bread crumbs   One half lemmon -- for juice

Cut fillets into nugget-sized pieces. Dip into mayonnaise and then into seasoned bread crumbs, to coat. Arrange on very lightly greased baking pan and place into pre-heated 350 degree oven for 20 to 25 minutes. Place on pre-warmed serving tray and sprinkle with lemon juice.

Cheese Sauce:
2 T. mayonnaise   1/2 cup coarsely grated
1 cup milk   cheese (cheddar is preferred,
                                            but any hard cheese is fine.)

Place all ingredients in pan and stir constantly until cheese is melted and sauce in bubbly. Spoon over fish nuggets and serve immediately.

BARBECUED FILLETS OR STEAKS
(Options: weakfish, bluefish, mackerel, porgy, tuna)

2 lbs. fillets or steaks
1/4 cup chopped onion
2 T. chopped green pepper
1 clove garlic, finely chopped
2 T. oil
1 8 oz. can tomato sauce

3 T. lemon juice
1 T. Worcestershire sauce
1 T. sugar
2 tsp. salt
1 tsp . pepper

Cook onion, green pepper, and garlic in oil until tender. Add remaining ingredients, except fish, and simmer for 5 minutes, stirring occasionally. Put aside. Cut fish into 6 portions. Place fish in a single layer in a baking dish. Pour sauce over fish and let stand for 30 minutes, turning fish once. Remove fish, reserving sauce for basting. Place fish in well-greased hinged wire grill. Cook about four inches from moderately hot coals for 5 to 8 minutes. Baste with sauce. Turn. Cook for 5 to 8 minutes longer or until fish flakes easily when tested with a fork. Serves 6.

FLORENTINE FILLETS
(Options: blackfish, sea bass, porgy)

1 lb. fillets
1 10-oz. pkg. frozen chopped
   spinach
1 3-oz. pkg. cream cheese,
   softened
1 T. margarine
4 tsp. flour

1/8 tsp. salt
Dash pepper
1 chicken bouillon cube
   dissolved in 3/4 cup water
   (Fish stock may be substituted)
Paprika

Cook and drain spinach. Place in bottom of 1 1/2 qt. casserole dish. Cut fillets into four pieces. Spoon a little cheese onto each piece of fish (use only half the cheese for this). Now roll up each piece of fish. Season with salt and pepper. Place fish on top of spinach.

Melt margarine and mix in flour, salt and pepper. Slowly add bouillon to make sauce. Melt in remaining cheese, cook and stir until thick. Pour sauce over fillets. Sprinkle with paprika. Bake uncovered at 350 degrees for 20 to 25 minutes. Serves three.

RED HOT BLACKFISH
(Options: sea bass, striped bass, bluefish, porgy)

2 lbs. fillets	1/2 T. chili powder
2 T. oil	1/2 chopped garlic clove
2 T. soy sauce	2 Dashes tabasco sauce
3 T. Worcestershire sauce	1/4 tsp. black pepper
1 T. paprika	

Place fillets, not touching, in a well-greased ovenproof baking pan. Combine all remaining ingredients and pour this sauce over fillets. Broil four inches from heat for approximately five minutes. Baste, turn, and baste again. Broil until fish flakes easily. Serve with lemon wedges.

FISH FLORENTINE WITH OYSTERS
(Options: cod, haddock, hake, halibut, sea bass, striped bass, black-fish, fluke)

1 lb. fillets or steaks	1/4 cup white wine
1 pint shucked oysters (reserve all liquid)	1 10 oz. pkg. frozen chopped spinach
1 T. softened butter or mar-garine	1 egg yolk
	Juice of 1/4 lemon

Arrange fish in small buttered baking dish. Spread softened margarine over fish, pour on the wine then lightly salt and pepper. Cover with foil and bake 15 minutes at 400 degrees, basting twice. Cook spinach and drain well. Return it to pot to keep warm and add a little butter.

Poach oysters with lemon juice and salt and pepper in their own juice until edges curl. Drain oysters. Return oyster poaching liquid to same pan and add juices of fish fillets from baking dish; reduce to half original volume.

Sauce:

2 T. butter or margarine	1 cup hot milk
1 1/2 T. flour	Salt & pepper

Stir flour into melted butter until smooth then add milk and beat. Add oysters and reduced pan liquid and beat into sauce. Whisk in egg yolk. Stir well.

Add the spinach over the fillets in the original baking dish and top with sauce. Broil six inches from heat for 3 minutes. Serves 4.

GOLDEN FISH BAKE
(Options: cod, haddock, pollack, hake, sea bass, striped bass, blackfish)

1 1/2 lbs. fillets	2/3 cup milk
1/4 cup butter or margarine	4 slices American cheese
10 3/4 oz. can golden mushroom soup	Salt & pepper to taste

Crust:
2 cups Bisquick baking mix
2/3 cup milk

Dill weed (optional)

Cut the fish into two-inch square pieces. Saute in margarine for two to three minutes. Salt and pepper to taste. Combine the soup and milk; mix well. Place sauteed fish into baking dish. Pour soup mixture over the fish. Lay cheese slices on top. Prepare the crust by mixing together Bisquick and milk until a soft dough forms. Drop by tablespoons onto top of casserole mixture until completely covered. Sprinkle with a pinch of dill weed, if desired. Bake uncovered in a 400 degree oven for 25-30 minutes or until golden. Serves 6.

DEEP SEA PARMAGIANA
(Options: cod, haddock, pollack, hake, large bluefish, blackfish)

2 lbs. fish steak or fillet	1 1/2 cups dry bread crumbs
1/2 cup all-purpose flour	1/2 cup cooking oil
1/2 tsp. salt	1 jar (16 oz.) tomato sauce
1/4 tsp. garlic powder	1 1/2 cups grated mozzarella cheese
1/4 tsp. oregano	
1 egg	1/4 cup parmesan cheese
1 T. water	

Combine flour, salt, garlic, and oregano in shallow dish or pan. Break egg into a second pan. Add water, and beat thoroughly with a fork. In a third pan place bread crumbs. Cover fish with flour, then dip in egg mixture, being sure to moisten both sides. Roll fish in bread crumbs. In large skillet, heat oil over medium high heat. Saute fish, cooking 3 minutes per side, or until golden brown. Place in baking dish; cover with mozzarella cheese, then tomato sauce. Sprinkle with parmesan cheese. Bake at 425 degrees for 15 to 20 minutes. Serves 6

ABOUT THE AUTHOR

A member of the *Outdoor Writers Association of America*, Tom Schlichter has been writing professionally for over six years. He has extensively covered both fresh and salt water fishing in newspapers and magazines including *Sports Afield, The Fisherman, Boy's Life, Long Island Outdoors*, and *The Fire Island Tide*.

As Suffolk County, New York, leader for the Cooperative Extension — 4-H Sportfishing Program and advisor to the Cooperative Extension — Sea Grant Master Angler Program, Tom has introduced youngsters and adults alike to the pleasures of angling.